Desperate for
Hope

Hanging On and Finding God
during Life's Hardest Times

BRUCE W. MARTIN

Revell

a division of Baker Publishing Group
Grand Rapids, Michigan

© 2012 by Bruce W. Martin

Published by Revell
a division of Baker Publishing Group
P.O. Box 6287, Grand Rapids, MI 49516-6287
www.revellbooks.com

Printed in the United States of America

Library of Congress Cataloging-in-Publication Data
Martin, Bruce W.
    Desperate for hope : hanging on and finding God during life's hardest times / Bruce W. Martin.
        p.   cm.
    ISBN 978-0-8007-2054-4 (pbk.)
        1. Suffering—Religious aspects—Christianity. 2. Hope—Religious aspects—Christianity. I. Title.
    BV4909.M36 2012
    248.8′6—dc23   2012012560

To protect the privacy of those who have shared their stories with the author, some details and names have been changed.

The internet addresses, email addresses, and phone numbers in this book are accurate at the time of publication. They are provided as a resource. Baker Publishing Group does not endorse them or vouch for their content or permanence.

In keeping with biblical principles of creation stewardship, Baker Publishing Group advocates the responsible use of our natural resources. As a member of the Green Press Initiative, our company uses recycled paper when possible. The text paper of this book is composed in part of post-consumer waste.

12   13   14   15   16   17   18   7   6   5   4   3   2

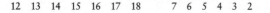

This book is lovingly dedicated to my wife Marlina, who has journeyed with me through the pain of infertility, failed adoptions, and broken dreams. Thank you for blessing me to be away for weeks at a time to write, and for putting up with me for twenty-eight years now. Your smile still lights up a room. God has remembered you!

Contents

Contents

Acknowledgments

First and foremost, I want to thank my heavenly Father who loves me fiercely enough to allow suffering, the Holy Spirit who has been my great Comfort and Counselor in suffering, and Jesus Christ who modeled suffering and has been with me every step of the way.

I believe a book is never birthed by one person but by many. As such, I have a lot of people to thank for this one. Mom and Dad, thank you for praying for me every day and for modeling what it means to follow Christ. To Austin Boyd, thank you for believing in me enough to mentor me through the writing process. To Mary DeMuth, thank you for helping me grow as a writer. To Vicki Crumpton, thank you for taking a chance on a beginner and for being so gracious through the writing process! To Krista, thank you for insisting that I "Write it!" To Mark, Roy, and Bobby, thank you for being such good friends during my seasons of suffering. To Roger, thank you for joining me on writing breaks and being a friend "who sticks closer than a brother." To Mark, Wendy, Jonathan, Betsy, Jessica, and Daniel, thank you for sharing your lives with me. You are precious friends. To my son, Zachary, thank you for being patient with an imperfect dad and for reminding me every day of the goodness of God.

Introduction

I still remember the phone call five days before Christmas 2002. A sinking feeling grew in my stomach as I realized who the caller was. I knew instinctively how the call would go. As my wife pleaded with the young girl on the other end of the line, desperation in her voice, I felt helpless and a little embarrassed. Her voice trembled.

"Don't do this. Please don't do this to our family!"

We were losing our daughter.

We'd been down this road before. Several years before, we'd lost twin boys in a failed adoption attempt. And now the nightmare was replaying itself. Only worse. This time, we'd brought her home. For the last ten weeks we had fallen in love with our first daughter, Zoe Marie. We had prayed and prayed for God to give us a second child, and he gave us a beautiful, strawberry blonde girl. For the first month, I successfully kept my heart at a distance. But after several weeks of feeding her, changing her, making her laugh, and comforting her when she cried, I was hooked. I would hold her for hours at a time and just stare at her face. Awake or asleep, it didn't matter. I was her father and she was my princess.

But our dream shattered. The birthmother had changed her mind, and we would have to give her back. We had no legal recourse. We knew this was a possibility, but our lawyer really thought she would sign the paperwork. She just needed a little time.

Ten weeks.

Now I faced the impossible task of comforting my wife. The desperation I heard in her voice as she begged for her child didn't bode well for me. As hard as losing another child was going to be for me, it was going to be even harder on her.

And how was I going to explain to my four-year-old son that he didn't have a sister anymore? I didn't even want to think about it.

The timing couldn't have been worse. Out of work, I hadn't received a paycheck for sixteen of the previous twenty-four months. We had just moved back to Huntsville, Alabama, from Denver, Colorado, after a colossal failure at church-planting. Drowning in a sea of credit card debt, we lived about thirty days from bankruptcy. To top it all off, my wife and I both suffered from near-clinical depression. At the lowest point of my life, the one bright spot was Zoe.

The Perfect Storm

That phone call culminated our "perfect storm." Three individual storms collided in our lives at the same time with devastating results. We thought we were going to die. And to be honest, that would've been fine with me. I was tired. Tired of the pain. Tired of trying to do the right thing and getting nothing but disappointment. Tired of saying the right thing, propping up my family with a seemingly unlimited supply of optimism and spiritual fortitude. Tired of serving God.

I was done.

Maybe you can relate. It's amazing to me how a single phone call can ruin your life. Things are going just fine, and then the call comes.

There's been an accident.

There's a mass in your breast.

The company's downsizing.

Your husband is leaving.

Your daughter was raped.

And all of a sudden your life is spinning out of control.

I was in the room with good friends when one of those calls came. We were all playing cards together on a Saturday night, when the father's cell phone rang. He recognized the number immediately and smiled as he prepared to talk to his daughter, who was away at her first year in college. She probably just needed a little extra spending cash.

He should be so lucky.

The smile faded and his face turned grave and ashen as he got the news every father hopes he'll never hear: his precious daughter had been raped. Her mother burst into tears as she heard the conversation unfold. From across the table, I could hear the daughter's voice—ashamed, uncertain, and afraid. Very afraid. Not simply of the perpetrator, but of what her future held.

What man could ever love her now? She was tainted. Used. Trash.

My friend bravely kept his voice steady as he tried to reassure her and assess the situation. Had she been to the doctor? Had she been to the police? Were there any witnesses? We'll be there as soon as we can.

It was surreal.

One minute we're all playing cards, talking and laughing and enjoying a friendship forged from more than twenty years together.

The next minute, everybody's crying.

Our friends were in shock, and my wife and I were racking our brains, trying to think of anything that might console them. But what do you say? We're sorry? It'll be okay? God's going to help out?

The silence was deafening.

Suffering is a universal experience. At some point, we've all felt the pain of loss, bitter disappointment, embarrassing failure, unthinkable betrayal, and the seeming randomness of suffering. Some of us have faced death. And we have quietly wondered (or maybe even screamed), "Why is this happening to me? Where is God in all of this?"

The answer may surprise you.

The Truth about Suffering

What you hold in your hand is a book about hope in the face of suffering. But more than that, it's a book about truth, sometimes disturbing truth, that at first glance seems discomforting. But I've learned over the years that there is a certain kind of comfort that can only be found on the other side of truth. The mother who gets the call that her son is missing in action will never be comforted or find any real healing until she knows what happened to her son, as painful as that truth might be.

God understands our quest for truth in suffering. Since ancient times, humans have asked, "Why do bad things happen to good people?" In one of the oldest books of the Bible, the book of Job, God pulls back the curtain and gives us a glimpse of what's going on behind the scenes of tragedy and hardship. But the answers we find there are more than a little disturbing.

They're true, but probably not what we expected.

Throughout this book, we'll tell Job's story—a true story about suffering and loss on an epic scale. But it's also a true story about hope. In fact, the word *hope* is used more times in Job than in any other book of the Bible except the Psalms. But you need to know this about hope going in: it doesn't come quickly. There's one other word that's used more in Job than any other book of the Bible except the Psalms.

The word *wait*.

Hope waits.

In addition to Job's story, we'll hear the real-life stories of others who've endured unthinkable tragedy and seek to learn from their experience. People who've lost children to shipwreck and disease, who've lost all of their earthly possessions to fire, who've lost their dreams to cancer and its aftermath. I'll also share my story about our family's painful struggle with infertility, the loss of children, career failures, depression, and near-bankruptcy.

In all of these stories, I pray that you'll find hope.

Webster's dictionary defines *hope* with these words: "to desire with expectation of fulfillment." Wherever you are in the journey of suffering, I pray that God will awaken in you a "desire with expectation of fulfillment."

More than that, I pray you'll encounter Jesus Christ, who describes himself as the Truth. Because we're not simply desperate for hope.

We're desperate for truth.

PART 1

The Divine Setup

I bring prosperity and create disaster;

I, the Lord, *do all these things.*

— Isaiah 45:7 —

1

You Want Answers?

I've long been fascinated by the true story in the bestselling book *The Perfect Storm* by Sebastian Junger. My first introduction to it was the blockbuster movie with the same title, and I later bought the book and wasn't disappointed. It's the fateful story of the crew of the fishing boat *Andrea Gail* and their final voyage on the high seas.

In fall 1991, Captain Billy Tyne gathered a group of fishermen and headed out to sea for a late-season swordfish catch. While they were at sea, a series of storms gathered and collided over the Eastern Seaboard of the United States, creating a cataclysmic weather system dubbed by the National Weather Service as "The Perfect Storm." This was a highly unusual storm because of the way it formed. It started with a hurricane that meandered around in the Atlantic Ocean. This hurricane was weakened and absorbed by an approaching cold front moving over the New England area. The third storm resulted from a growing low pressure system off Sable Island, part of the province of Nova Scotia. The bizarre combination of these three weather systems formed one massive storm that exploded over the Atlantic Ocean and pummeled the New England states. The damage? In the hundreds of millions, with thirteen counties declared federal disaster areas.

The six fishermen aboard the *Andrea Gail* never returned.

I have also been fascinated by another true story that mirrors this one. A guy named Matthew tells it in the bestselling book the Bible. Turns out, he was an eyewitness to the event. Somewhere around 30 AD, a captain by the name of Jesus gathered a group of men around him and led them out to sea, determined to take them to a new place. And he led them straight into the heart of a storm. They never returned . . . not the same, anyway.

It goes like this.

> When Jesus saw the crowd around him, he gave orders to cross to the other side of the lake. . . . Then he got into the boat and his disciples followed him. Without warning, a furious storm came up on the lake, so that the waves swept over the boat. But Jesus was sleeping. The disciples went and woke him, saying, "Lord, save us! We're going to drown!" (Matt. 8:18, 23–25)

Great story, huh? It's amazing how many times I've read that story and missed a lot of really important stuff. Probably because I was more interested in the end of the story—you know, where Jesus miraculously calms the storm and everything is hunky-dory again. I think that's just human nature. *Skip to the end,* I think. *Just get me to the other side of the storm. Tell me the happy ending. I want to know how it all works out.*

And as a result, I miss much of what God wants to teach me in the process. There are several mildly disturbing things about this story that I need to point out before we move on.

Okay, for starters, who led them into the storm? Scripture says that Jesus gave the order for everyone to follow him into the boat. So Jesus, God incarnate, led them right into the storm. And apparently he didn't bother to mention anything about said storm, because "Without warning, a furious storm came up."

Now, I'm thinking it would've been nice for Jesus to at least let his disciples know a storm was brewing. Better yet, how about they not take the boat at all? They could always walk around instead. But no, Jesus brought them right into the heart of a furious storm that was so bad it convinced seasoned fishermen they were all going to die.

In my experience, the worst storms that come into our lives generally arrive without warning. A loved one receives a cancer diagnosis. We lose our jobs, sometimes through no fault of our own. We find out we can't get pregnant. We find out that our teenage daughter is pregnant. A good friend betrays us. Or, perhaps worst of all, death snatches a child or a spouse. And in one moment, our lives reel out of control.

But that isn't the most disturbing thing for me in this story. Not by a long shot. It's the whole "but Jesus was sleeping" thing. I find that highly disturbing. Even wrong. How do you sleep through a storm like that? Particularly when you've got the power to stop it!

Have you ever felt this way? That you were (or are) going through the worst storm of your life, and it feels like God is sleeping? *Why doesn't he do something? Why doesn't he stop it? Can't he see that I'm in pain?*

I have.

Here's what I am learning about God: God is more intent on perfecting us through trouble than on protecting us from trouble.

The Scripture passage that inspired this whole book is James 1:2–4:

> Consider it all joy, my brethren, when you encounter various trials, knowing that the testing of your faith produces endurance. And let endurance have its perfect result, that you may be perfect and complete, lacking in nothing. (NASB)

Here's my paraphrase on that:

> If you are a child of God, you can have joy when you experience major storms in life because you know a secret! Every time you endure a storm, your faith is being strengthened and God is making you perfect, just like Jesus Christ. (MBT—Modern Bruce Translation)

God is intent on making us perfect. Not just good—perfect. God is not as interested in making our lives pleasant as he is in making our lives perfect.

This may not be exactly what you want to hear. But it's true. Don't put this book down just yet though. There are far more disturbing realities to come.

God is more intent on perfecting us through trouble than on protecting us from trouble.

Here's what I love about that storm story from Matthew 8: Jesus hung with them—before the storm, in the storm, and after the storm. It reminds me of the final words of Jesus before he ascended into heaven and turned the whole thing over to us: "Surely I am with you always, to the very end of the age" (Matt. 28:20). We often miss the amazing comfort and strength found in those words. Our prayers frequently reflect that we're more interested in God's presents than in his presence.

I know mine do.

But the older I get, and the more storms I endure, the more I realize the incredible importance of the truth that God is always with me. No matter what. And that is enough.

I am never alone. And neither are you.

Here's something else I find comforting: Jesus also had to endure perfect storms. They were part of his perfect journey too. Scripture records this in Hebrews 2:10: "In bringing many sons to glory, it was fitting that God, for whom and through whom everything exists, should make the author of their salvation perfect through suffering."

Jesus suffered storms. Bad ones. Scripture describes Jesus as "a man of sorrows, and acquainted with grief" (Isa. 53:3 KJV). The writer of Hebrews says that we do not have a Savior who "cannot be touched with the feeling of our infirmities" (Heb. 4:15 KJV).

He's been there. He knows what it feels like. And he'll be there for us.

But that doesn't mean we won't have questions.

Typically there are two questions that form when storms hit. The first one is generally, "What am I going to do?" When a storm hits without warning, we jump into an "all hands on deck" mode and get very busy with doing something about it. For most of us, that usually includes prayer at some level. We are wired to try and fix the problem. To overcome it. To find shelter. To find relief.

But somewhere after we begin to come to grips with what is happening, we ask what is perhaps a larger, scarier question born out of a nagging feeling that we've been deceived in some way, maybe even betrayed. By God.

This second question rises up, almost unconsciously, from the deep recesses of our soul: "WHY?"

Why is a storm coming into my life?

Why do bad things happen to good people like me?

Why does God allow (or, heaven forbid, even cause) suffering?

Why doesn't God relieve my pain?

Why doesn't he fix this?

These are age-old questions and book after book have explored this theme. They are legitimate questions with legitimate answers. But many of the answers to these questions are not obvious. There are some obvious ones, to be sure, and we'll acknowledge those.

But there are others, even more profound, that hide. Better said, these answers are obscured, often by their more obvious counterparts. These more profound answers are where we will spend the majority of our time in this book.

There are many reasons why storms come into our lives. We'll divide the answers to the "WHY?" questions into two categories:

1. Obvious reasons
2. Not so obvious reasons

Simple enough. In case you haven't figured it out yet, the "not so obvious reasons" will be the more profound ones.

Here we go.

Your Story

How do you feel about the statement "God is more intent on perfecting us through trouble than he is on protecting us from trouble"? Be honest.

Have you ever felt that Jesus was distant, sort of "asleep in the boat" when you were going through something difficult?

Have you ever felt yourself questioning the goodness of God in the face of trouble?

What are some questions you'd like to have answered in relation to your suffering? Take time to write them down now as we begin this journey together.

2

A Bad Call

Let's just start with the most obvious reason storms come, and get it out of the way.

Obvious Reason #1: You Made a Bad Call!

Okay, this is a no-brainer. You made a bad decision. Maybe you made an unwise choice that didn't seem like it was going to be such a big deal. Or maybe you just outright rebelled against God.

Either way you're in a storm, and you know it is a storm of your own making. In some ways, this makes it all the more painful. You feel regret. *If only I had done such and such*. It's bad and it was avoidable.

The story of Jonah fits this category. He received a clear directive from God to go to Nineveh with a specific message. It wasn't like he could have been unsure about what God wanted. He just flat out didn't want to do it.

So this bright boy jumped on a ship going the opposite direction. Bad call. This is what God calls sin. And guess what?

Jonah sailed right into a furious storm! And he knew exactly why. When everyone else on board cried out, "Why?" he stepped forward and, in his best Bob Newhart impression, said, "That uh . . . that would be me." This was a storm of his own making. He was responsible and he knew it.

Not So Obvious Reason #1: God Is Crazy about You!

This may seem a little counterintuitive. When you end up in a storm you have caused, it feels as though God is somehow mad at you and dislikes you. But the opposite is true! God brings discipline into our lives because he is crazy about us. He delights in us.

Proverbs 3:11–12 says, "My son, do not despise the LORD's discipline and do not resent his rebuke, because the LORD disciplines those he loves, as a father the son he delights in." If you are undergoing hardship as a result of sin, know this: God delights in you!

I've made my share of bad decisions. More than my share, in fact. There was a time not that long ago when I made a series of terrible decisions. As the pastor of a growing church, during a time of stress and anxiety, I made some horrible choices. They were wrong and I knew it. No excuses.

When I confessed my sin to the elders and then the congregation, it blew up the whole church. I insisted that it be handled publicly, not covered up or swept under the rug. It was the right thing to do. However, I misjudged the fallout. My confession hurt a lot of people, and caused a lot of disillusionment and disappointment. Retrospectively, my confession and its resulting fallout became one of the worst storms I have ever navigated.

I ended up resigning from the church I had planted seven years earlier. It was one of the hardest decisions I ever made, but the fallout from my sin led me to believe I could no longer serve there effectively. But what to do now?

We had done some research on Denver, Colorado, and determined it needed church planters in a bad way. Some 93 percent of its residents were unchurched. Our plan was to resign our existing church, spend the next three months or so raising money, then move to Colorado early the following year.

The day I resigned was September 10, 2001. The following day, the world was changed forever with the attack on the World Trade Center. With the rest of America, my congregation was emotionally devastated by the attack, but now it was without a pastor to help them navigate the uncertainties that day brought. I felt like a total loser, like a shepherd who deserted the sheep right when the wolf attacked. I was torn. Part of me wanted to go back and plead with our elders to reinstate me as pastor. The other part of me wanted to run far away as fast as I could. Just get to Denver, start over, and try to get the ship righted again.

I took a short-term manual labor job just to help pay the bills while I tried unsuccessfully to raise money for this new church-planting venture. It just wasn't there. 9/11 created so much economic uncertainty that neither churches nor businesses were able to commit to a new church plant. But I felt like I had to get out of the city, so we moved to Denver anyway.

Things went from bad to worse at that point. We didn't have any money raised, so I began trying to get some part-time work that would allow me to do church planting on the side. But work was hard to find and we ended up living on our credit cards.

Not a good plan.

We moved back to Huntsville after just four months. It was embarrassing on so many levels.

I was a wreck. I lapsed into a severe state of depression and became reclusive. Having to look people in the eye and make conversation was just too painful. I only interacted with close friends, but even then, I didn't tell anyone where I was emotionally. I felt a combination of guilt, sadness, anger, and frustration every single day. I wasn't angry with God, but I was furious with myself. *How could I have let it come to this? What's wrong with me? Stupid, stupid, stupid!*

I had disappointed so many people: myself, my wife, my friends, our church. But even worse, I felt as if God was disappointed in me, even angry with me. In the midst of all this self-loathing and regret, the only prayer I felt like I could pray was, "I'm so sorry. Please forgive me." I could relate to the story of the prodigal son in Luke 15 who made some terrible choices in relation to his dad. His thought process was, *I've blown it so bad, I'm not even worthy to be called your son. Just make me a slave in your household.*

Check that box.

Now here's where it got weird for me. At possibly the lowest point in my life in terms of guilt and regret, God spoke to me. Clearly. In a mall.

I love you!

I was sitting in the middle of a mall in Huntsville, Alabama. No, really, more like lying down. You have to understand, malls make me tired. Seriously. Physically tired. I literally yawn as I walk through the front door. I typically avoid malls at all costs, unless there's something good at the food court.

But my wife wanted to do some shopping and I wanted to be with her, so I went to the dreaded mall. I didn't actually go in the stores though. I found one of the big open areas in the middle of the mall and stretched out on a couch right underneath a huge domed skylight. As I began to fall asleep, I remember praying something along the lines of "I'm so sorry" again. And I heard it.

I love you!

Come again?

I love you and I'm not disappointed with you.

I didn't see that coming.

For the next five minutes as I sat on that couch, bathed in sunlight streaming in from the skylight, I sensed (for lack of a better word) wave after wave after wave of God's love pouring over, into, and through my body and soul.

I love you. I love you. I love you.

I've never forgotten that moment.

Here's part of what God showed me during that season: he delights in me, as a father delights in his son! He's never disappointed *in* me. I'm his beloved son! There are certainly times that he is disappointed *for* me, because he knows the decision I'm making isn't going to serve me well. But he's never disappointed with me.

This is such a beautiful reality if you are willing to accept it. It's the essence of the gospel. God doesn't treat us as our sins deserve! It's not as though, "He likes us when we do right and dislikes us when we do wrong." No. He simply loves us. All the time.

Later, as I reflected on that experience with God in the mall, I remembered something. For years at our church I had been telling people that God loved them. That God was crazy about them! No matter how far they had strayed from him, no matter what sins they had committed, God loved them. And in a beautiful way, people had responded. I had watched person after person receive God's love and forgiveness.

But I hadn't. Not really.

All those years I had preached that God loved people no matter what. But what I realized later was this: never once, in seven years of preaching and teaching, did I ever publicly acknowledge that God loved *me* no matter what.

I didn't believe it.

Don't get me wrong. I knew John 3:16 and everything. You know, for God so loved the world . . . and all that. And I was part of the world, so by default, God loved me. I knew that at an intellectual, impersonal level. I just struggled to believe it. I was so aware of my sin and shortcomings that I think I was always unconsciously trying to earn God's love. So when I blew it, I couldn't help but feel that God loved me less—that he was profoundly disappointed and even displeased with me.

Sometime during that season, I read in 2 Samuel the story of David committing adultery with Bathsheba and then murdering her husband. Pretty bad stuff. I mean, gee, I hadn't gone that far. But in the very last verse of chapter 11, it says that God was displeased with the thing David had *done*.

I should think so. Adultery. Murder. These would make the top ten on most people's list.

But then I noticed this: it didn't say that God was displeased with *David*, only with what he had done. What he *did* was sinful. But God was not displeased with David. God loved David with an everlasting love. This is why David says later in Psalms,

> He does not treat us as our sins deserve
>   or repay us according to our iniquities.
> For as high as the heavens are above the earth,
>   so great is his love for those who fear him.
>   (Ps. 103:10–11)

David recognized that the love of God was greater than his sin. And he received that love.

By the way, adulterers and murderers were supposed to be stoned. That's what the law required. That's what justice demanded. But neither David nor Bathsheba were stoned. And that's the essence of the gospel—mercy triumphs over justice! David knew firsthand how great the love of God was for him.

Don't get me wrong—I'm not saying there weren't any consequences for his sin. The consequences of his sin were incredibly painful. David lost a son as a result. Long-term, he lost four sons. But he never lost the love and presence of God.

In the same way, God is never disappointed in you! There are times when God is disappointed *for* you when you make a bad decision, but he is never disappointed in you. You are his beloved child! So when you're experiencing painful consequences as the result of sin, know this: God loves you.

And he loves you too much to let you go your own way. This is why he brings discipline into our lives.

The writer of Hebrews refers to this truth.

You have forgotten that word of encouragement that addresses you as sons:

> "My son, do not make light of the Lord's discipline,
>   and do not lose heart when he rebukes you,
> because the Lord disciplines those he loves,
>   and he punishes everyone he accepts as a son."

Endure hardship as discipline; God is treating you as sons. For what son is not disciplined by his father? If you are not disciplined (and everyone undergoes discipline), then you are illegitimate children and not true sons. Moreover, we have all had human fathers who disciplined us and we respected them for it. How much more should we submit to the Father of our spirits and live! Our fathers disciplined us for a little while as they thought best; but God disciplines us for our good, that we may share in his holiness [or perfection]. No discipline seems pleasant at the time, but painful. Later on, however, it produces a harvest of righteousness and peace for those who have been trained by it. (Heb. 12:5–11)

God disciplines you and me because he loves us and because he delights in us!

I have a son named Zachary. He's my only child and I'm crazy about him. As a result, I hate having to discipline him. But I know that I have to or he will never grow and develop maturity and good character. And I love him too much to stunt his growth.

When he started kindergarten at age five, he went to a school that employed an unfortunate system of discipline in the form of a series of "conduct necklaces." Here's how it worked: you started every day with a green necklace. If you were "good" all day long, you got to keep your green necklace and wear it home. However, if you had some trouble that day, such as talking out of turn, getting out of your seat, or not following instructions, then you would receive a yellow warning necklace to wear home. This let your parents (and everyone else) know you were "on probation." But if you were really "bad," you know, like hitting someone, or dissing the teacher, you got a red necklace. The proverbial "scarlet letter" of the kindergarten world.

Well, the first day, Zachary came home with a green necklace and I thought, *That's my boy!* On days two and three, still a green necklace. *I am such a good parent*, I congratulated myself. Another pastor's kid who went to the same school came home with a yellow necklace, and I thought to myself, *That's too bad. They've got some parenting work to do there. You know a church leader has to be able to manage his own household.*

Day four rolled around, and my son didn't sport a green necklace.

Or a yellow one.

Nope, he went straight to red! Why bother with a warning necklace? Let's just embarrass Mom and Dad to death and stroll out of the school with a red one, a glaring, crimson indictment of their parenting prowess!

Okay, but anyone can have a bad day, right? So I had a little discussion with Zachary, knowing my parental words of wisdom would turn his little life around.

At least until Friday.

Red necklace again.

Where did I go wrong? How could he do this to me?

My five-year-old son was on the road to perdition. I readied myself to go off on him. No words of wisdom this time. Just a fierce tongue-lashing followed by the requisite spanking.

I'll never forget what he said to me as he got in the car that day. He looked up at me with his sad, repentant little eyes and said, "I knew you'd be mad at me."

Okay, so the tongue-lashing was out.

In fact it broke my heart. Sadly, it was a painful reminder of my typical parenting style when Zach messed up: anger.

Tears formed as I scooped him into my arms. "I'm not mad at you. I'm crazy about you!" I said, telling him what God had told me several years earlier. "Zachary, I'm never disappointed in you. I'm sometimes disappointed for you because I know you're making a bad decision. But you are never a disappointment to me. I love you! The reason I discipline you is because I love you too much to let you go your own way."

I did have to spank him. There was still a consequence for his sin. But it wasn't in anger.

I love the scene from the movie *Evan Almighty* when Evan is being doused by the sprinkler system in his front yard. He looks up and says to God, "I know that whatever you do, you do because you love me. But could you love me a little bit less?"

Zach felt the same way that day. And I have felt that way too. There is no discipline that seems pleasant at the time, just painful. It can actually feel like you are unloved. But the opposite is true. It proves God's love for us.

So endure the storm. Stay the course. Don't give up. In due time, God will lift you up and bring a harvest of righteousness and peace into your life. He's perfecting you!

By the way, he's not just perfecting you for your benefit. He's also perfecting you for the benefit of others.

Which brings us to the next obvious reason that storms come into our lives.

Your Story

Have you ever felt like God was deeply disappointed, maybe even angry with you, because of your sin?

Look back on your life. Have you experienced a "harvest of righteousness" or a "harvest of peace" after you endured the painful consequences of a bad decision?

Is there any area of your life right now where, like Jonah, you know you're headed in the wrong direction? It's not too late to turn around!

How does it feel to know that you are loved deeply by God, that God delights in you, even when you sin? Do you believe that?

3

Collateral Damage

One of the first things we focus on when something bad happens is ourselves. *What did I do to deserve this?* And more often than not, the answer is nothing. You didn't do anything wrong.

Someone else did.

Which is the next most obvious reason storms come.

Obvious Reason #2: Someone Else Made a Bad Call

This is a tough pill to swallow, but sometimes you are enduring a storm someone else stirred up. You just happened to be in close enough proximity that their storm became yours. This could be a spouse, a co-worker, a boss, a parent, a child, a sibling, and so forth. Someone blew it, and now you're reaping the consequences of their sin.

Your wife committed adultery and now you've got a sexually transmitted disease.

Your boss made a bad decision and now everyone's out of a job.

Your husband did something illegal and went to prison for it, and now you're faced with financial ruin.

A drunk driver ran a red light and killed your child.

Your daughter was raped and will have to endure a lifetime of emotional scars.

Collateral damage. Someone else sins, but you're reaping the consequences.

In this situation, many succumb to bitterness because of the unfairness factor. *Why should my life have to be destroyed because of what someone else did? Why didn't God prevent this from happening?* Or at least, *Why didn't God protect me from the consequences?*

One of the reasons we must take sin seriously is because of its collateral damage. As much as I hate to admit it, some of my bad decisions have caused major storms for others. My sin wounded people I cared about, including my wife, my family, and the church where I served. It would be almost impossible to live with—except for the fact that I know something from the "not so obvious" category.

Not So Obvious Reason #2: God Is Preparing You for Something

God is always up to something. Write that down. Memorize that statement. It's one of the more profound truths in this book. God is always up to something. And because he's good, that something will always be good. No matter how bad the storm is, and no matter who caused it, God is at work. It might look to you like he is sleeping, but he's at work behind the scenes.

The story of Joseph in the Old Testament fits this category well. Joseph was a young man with some incredible dreams for his life. His dad was particularly fond of him and made a significant investment in his wardrobe. Joseph looked good, and so did his future. His whole life stretched out before him, beckoning him to greatness.

But a storm was brewing. The rest of the family didn't appreciate his dreams—particularly his brothers. As a result of their jealousy, they made a series of bad decisions, starting with throwing Joseph into a pit and leaving him for dead.

God is always up to something.

Not good.

But the oldest brother starts feeling a little bad about the whole thing, so he talks the rest of them into selling their younger brother into slavery instead.

Slightly better than leaving him for dead, but not much.

However, while in slavery, Joseph makes the best out of a bad situation and works his way up to head slave, managing the entire household of his master, a guy named Potiphar. Again, not exactly what he'd dreamed about as a young man, but better than most slaves experience.

But then a second storm rolls in. Potiphar's wife has a "desperate housewives" moment and tries to seduce Joseph into sleeping with her. Joseph says no multiple times, and finally flees the house. To protect herself, Potiphar's wife concocts a story claiming that Joseph was trying to take advantage of her. Understandably, this doesn't sit real well with Potiphar, so he has Joseph thrown into prison.

As the result of another person's sin, this time Potiphar's wife, Joseph winds up in prison. For doing the right thing. He hadn't done anything wrong; he was simply reaping the whirlwind of other people's bad decisions.

Kind of redefines the meaning of collateral damage.

But even after he helped other prisoners gain their freedom during his time in prison, Joseph is forgotten, left for dead, rotting in a lonely prison cell.

Pretty much back to square one, when he was left for dead in the pit.

Don't you think Joseph had some questions? *Where is God in all of this? Why do bad things keep happening to me? I mean, I'm trying to do the right thing here. I'm actually avoiding sin and my life is getting progressively worse!*

Talk about the perfect storm. But God is always up to something.

Skillfully weaving all of these storms together—kidnapping, slavery, false accusations, and prison—God brings about ultimate good for Joseph, his family, and millions of others. In an incredible turn of events that only God could orchestrate, he positions Joseph as the second highest ranking leader in the nation.

So what is Joseph's take on his personal "storm of the century"?

God gives him an opportunity to confront the people who caused all of this misery in his life, and he says this:

> And now, do not be distressed and do not be angry with yourselves for selling me here, because it was to save lives that God sent me ahead of you. . . . God sent me ahead of you to preserve for you a remnant on earth and to save your lives by a great deliverance. So then, it was not you who sent me here, but God. . . . You intended to harm me, but God intended it for good to accomplish what is now being done, the saving of many lives. (Gen. 45:5–8; 50:20)

Later in his life, Joseph perceives the "not so obvious" reason for his storms: "a great deliverance . . . the saving of many lives." Interestingly enough, he credits God with bringing the storms!

A divine setup.

This probably wasn't Joseph's take during the middle of his storms. I imagine Joseph was a lot like you and me, crying out to God, "Why the pit, why the slavery, why the prison term?" And I don't think he got an answer. Not then. Only after the storm passed could he see the hand of God. God was preparing him for something great. But it took the perfect storm to carry him there.

Maybe you're in a storm someone else caused. In fact, it may be going a lot worse for you than it is for the person who made the bad decision! Don't allow yourself to become bitter. Forgive the person who caused the storm and know this: God is up to something! And he is preparing you for something. Something that will help others.

I heard a great quote recently by Frances Ridley Havergal: "God is preparing you for what he is preparing for you."

True that.

Your Story

When things go bad, it's normal to feel as if God is doing nothing. Are you willing, with eyes of faith, to believe that God is up to something good in your situation?

Have you ever found yourself in serious trouble for doing the right thing? How did you feel about God?

Can you see how God might be using hardship now to prepare you for something in the future?

God is able to take what others mean for evil and turn it into something good. Are you willing to forgive the person who caused you pain and trust God to bring good from it?

4

Stuff Happens

Generally speaking, if one of the first two reasons doesn't apply, we default to this one.

Obvious Reason #3: Stuff Happens!

It's pretty simple, really. We live in a fallen world and as such, bad things happen. Cancer strikes. A car accident kills a loved one. We lose our job because of corporate downsizing. We find out we can't have children. The list goes on and on.

The randomness of suffering can make us crazy. There's seemingly no reason for it. No one did anything wrong. We didn't bring this on ourselves. And no one brought it on us.

At least not that we can see.

In truth, stuff does happen for a reason. By that I mean someone or something causes it. In the natural realm, a storm doesn't form without something weather-related causing it to happen. A high pressure system meets a low pressure system. Warm, moist air from the Gulf meets a cold front from the north. There's a cause—and a storm rages.

In a similar way, storms enter our lives for a reason. They're not random. Something (or someone) causes them.

Not So Obvious Reason #3: We're Involved in a War

We are in the midst of a supernatural war. A spiritual battle.

God, speaking through Paul, puts it this way in Ephesians 6:12–13:

> For our struggle is not against flesh and blood, but against the rulers, against the authorities, against the powers of this dark world and against the spiritual forces of evil in the heavenly realms. Therefore put on the full armor of God, so that when the day of evil comes, you may be able to stand your ground.

Note the words he uses in this passage:

struggle
this dark world
spiritual forces of evil
the day of evil

Can you relate to those words? I can. I have seen my share of struggles. I have felt the influence of this dark world. I have sensed spiritual forces of evil at work. And the day of evil has visited my home more than once.

This is why life is so hard sometimes. It's not simply that bad stuff happens. There's more to it than that. It's the reality that we're born into a war, a heavenly war that's playing out on earth. The beautiful thing is that Jesus wasn't exempt from trouble when he came to earth. In fact, the story of the birth of Christ gives one of the most vivid examples of being born into a world at war.

Let's talk about the Christmas story for just a minute. Did you ever wonder why it had to be so hard for Mary and Joseph? Sometimes when we talk about that first Christmas it comes off as this beautiful, sweet little children's story. But it wasn't beautiful and sweet. It was horrendous!

Think about it.

For starters, Mary is a pregnant virgin. Pardon me? You want to try and explain that to your fiancé? Or your parents? Would've been nice to give Mom and Dad a little "heads-up" there. Then Mary and Joseph have to travel to a distant city to pay taxes. Great! It's the perfect way to start a marriage. "Let's take a long, expensive trip so we can give away money we don't have!" Oh, and then baby decides to come while they're out of town, away from family, friends . . . and midwives.

But certainly God has worked out a place for them to stay in Bethlehem, right? Guess again. There's no room for them in the inn. (I mean, it's not like God didn't know this was coming.) So Mary gives birth to her child away from her family, in a strange city, in a dark, dirty cave. Then she gets to put her newborn baby in a feeding trough.

It's just how she always pictured it.

Later on, Scripture records that Mary wondered about all these things in her heart. Here's what I think she might have been wondering about: *What the heck was that all about? Why does this have to be so hard? Where is God in all of this? Couldn't he have planned this out a little better?*

But it gets worse.

An angel wakes up Joseph in the middle of the night and tells him they have to move to Egypt. Right now. This instant. Why? Because someone's coming to kill their baby. I've tried to imagine Joseph explaining this to Mary.

Joseph: "Mary, wake up. We're moving to Egypt."

Mary: "Really? Are you serious? Can we talk about this in the morning?"

Joseph: "No, we have to leave right now! Pack your things."

Mary: "What? Why now? What's the rush?"

Joseph: "Someone's coming to kill the baby!"

What did Mary probably feel in that moment? Panic! Sheer terror. And probably a little irritation . . . with God. Couldn't he have given them a little more warning?

Again, why did it have to be so hard?

We have to go beyond the Gospel accounts to get the bigger picture. We have to go to the book of Revelation for a look behind the scenes at the spiritual reality. Here's a little different take on the Christmas story from Revelation 12, complete with dragons and demons!

> A great and wondrous sign appeared in heaven: a woman clothed with the sun, with the moon under her feet and a crown of twelve stars on her head. She was pregnant and cried out in pain as she was about to give birth. Then another sign appeared in heaven: an enormous red dragon with seven heads and ten horns and seven crowns on his heads. His tail swept a third of the stars out of the sky and flung them to the earth. The dragon stood in front of the woman who was about to give birth, so that he might devour her child the moment it was born. She gave birth to a son, a male child, who will rule all the nations with an iron scepter. And her child was snatched up to God and to his throne. The woman fled into the desert to a place prepared for her by God, where she might be taken care of for 1,260 days. (vv. 1–6)

Uh huh. Not exactly the version Linus quotes in Charlie Brown's Christmas special. But these verses are just an account from earth's perspective. Look at what was going on in heaven.

And there was war in heaven. Michael and his angels fought against the dragon, and the dragon and his angels fought back. But he was not strong enough, and they lost their place in heaven. The great dragon was hurled down—that ancient serpent called the devil, or Satan, who leads the whole world astray. He was hurled to the earth, and his angels with him. (vv. 7–9)

Great! God's team wins, right? Well, yes and no. The war in heaven has been won, but now the war comes to earth. The next several verses give a parallel story about the birth of the Church. In this parallel version, the dragon is still Satan, but the woman now represents the bride of Christ, the Church. As God births the Church at Pentecost, Satan immediately tries to kill it through intense persecution. But, by God's design, the Church flees and the gospel begins to spread to the ends of the earth.

Now, here's where our stories intersect, in verse 17. It's not pretty.

Then the dragon was enraged at the woman and went off to make war against the rest of her offspring—those who obey God's commandments and hold to the testimony of Jesus.

That would be us.

Satan's not happy and now he's making war against us. It's a little deeper than "stuff happens," isn't it?

Peter, a follower of Christ who knew firsthand what it was like to be in a world at war, said this: "Be self-controlled and alert. Your enemy the devil prowls around like a roaring lion looking for someone to devour" (1 Pet. 5:8). Peter had more than his fair share of run-ins with the devil, and was almost devoured!

This is serious business. You and I have a mortal enemy determined to ruin our lives and wreck our faith. And he'll use powerful storms to do his dirty work. Many of us are shocked when something bad happens. But in truth, we should be expecting it.

Francis Schaeffer put it this way:

> One cannot partake of [Jesus Christ] without being ready to see the world as a place of pilgrimage and war. . . . It is just plain stupid of a Christian not to expect spiritual warfare while he lives in enemy territory.[1]

I think that's a nice way of saying, "Don't be stupid." So how do we fight this battle?

Look at the next verse. "Resist him, standing firm in the faith" (1 Pet. 5:9). What's our battle plan? Resist him! Okay, but how do you resist an unseen enemy? By standing firm in your faith. By trusting God. We actually resist Satan by simply trusting God. Ultimately faith is always about trusting God, particularly when the day of evil comes.

And make no mistake. It will come.

Peter finishes the passage with these words:

> Because you know that your brothers throughout the world are undergoing the same kind of sufferings. And the God of all grace, who called you to his eternal glory in Christ, after you have suffered a little while, will himself restore you and make you strong, firm and steadfast. (vv. 9–10)

He reminds us that we're not alone in our suffering. Storms are raging for other believers all over the world. And he points us to the reality that there will be an end to our storm, "after you have suffered a little while."

1. Francis A. Schaeffer, *Joshua and the Flow of Biblical History* (Wheaton: Crossway, 2004), 87–88.

To be honest, that's not really encouraging to me. After all, a thousand years is like a day to God. How long might "a little while" be? I can't tell you. I don't know. But God does. And he'll use the storm to make you perfect.

By the way, did you notice that Peter refers to God as "the God of all grace" in that passage? It's a little disquieting to me to think that a gracious God would allow me to suffer for any length of time. I thought grace was a good thing. When I think of "the God of all grace," I'm thinking, "the God of all comfort," or, "the God of all peace," not so much "the God who allows suffering."

Ultimately faith is always about trusting God, particularly when the day of evil comes.

But in a way I don't fully understand, it is the grace of God that not only allows suffering but sometimes even initiates it.

Your Story

Did you ever think of the Christmas story as a war story? What are some of the questions Joseph and Mary must have had during their ordeal?

Why do you suppose God didn't "fix" everything and make it easier for them?

How do you feel about living in a "world at war"? Is it possible that you are in a significant battle right now?

Trusting God can seem passive, but it's the way we actively resist the devil. Where is God calling you to trust him right now?

5

The Problem with Grace

Here's a little trivia you probably don't know about the storm of the century. Do you recall what actually started the "Perfect Storm" in October 1991? As I mentioned earlier, the collision of three storms caused that massive storm, but it was a hurricane forming in the Atlantic Ocean that first initiated it. You want to take a wild guess at the name of that hurricane?

Grace.

Seriously. I'm not making this up.

Hurricane Grace. Ironic, isn't it? "The Perfect Storm," the storm of the century, was initiated by Grace.

In the same way, it's the grace of God that allows, *or even brings*, storms in our life. Remember, God is more intent on perfecting us through storms than protecting us from storms. There's a temptation to think that once we've experienced the grace of God in our life, the worst of our troubles are behind us. That once we make the decision to follow Jesus Christ, he will only lead us "beside the still waters." But this was not the case for the first followers of Jesus Christ, nor will it be so for us. There are certain things we can only learn by going through storms, and since God's intent on perfecting us, he'll insist that we experience them.

There's another storm Jesus and his disciples experienced that's told in three of the Gospels: Matthew 14, Mark 6, and John 6. Each Gospel account gives a unique perspective on the event, and when you combine all three accounts, you get a vivid picture of what the disciples encountered.

A much milder storm than the other one, this storm also boasted high winds and rough seas, but the disciples didn't think it would kill them. This storm story starts the same way as the other storm story—Jesus leads them into it.

Mark 6:45 records that "Jesus made his disciples get into the boat and go on ahead of him." This time, Jesus was not with them in the boat. No, he watched them from the shore. "He saw the disciples straining at the oars, because the wind was against them" (v. 48). He sees their struggle and decides to do something.

But this is where the story gets a little weird. "About the fourth watch of the night he went out to them, walking on the lake" (v. 48). Well that's pretty great. I mean, at least he's not sleeping! Jesus to the rescue, right? Not so much.

Look at the last part of the verse: "He was about to pass by them" (v. 48). You've got to be kidding me. He saw the disciples fighting the storm, miraculously walked on the water toward them, and then nearly passed them by like he was in a rush to get to the other side.

Have you ever felt like that in the middle of a storm? That God can see what's happening to you, but isn't doing anything about it? It's almost like Jesus is passing right by you, but not actually doing anything to help you with your trouble. What's up with that?

The disciples thought Jesus was a ghost and started screaming. Let's face it, you and I would too if we're in the middle of a storm at 3:00 a.m. and someone comes cruising across the water without a boat! But Jesus called out and told them who he was, and to have courage and not be afraid.

Interestingly enough though, he made no offer to help them or join them in the boat.

A Bizarre Invitation

Here's where the story gets weirder, perhaps even bizarre. Peter yells out to Jesus, "If it's really you, then tell me to come out there to you."

Does this strike you as a little bit odd? I can think of a lot of other things I would say there, like, "If it's really you, why don't you get in the boat and help us start rowing?" Or, better yet, "If it's really you, why don't you just say 'peace, be still' and end this storm like you did the other one?" But no, Peter tells Jesus to invite him out of the boat to join him on the water.

Perhaps the greatest miracles God works in our lives come during the worst times.

So Jesus said, "Come on!" I love this. Jesus doesn't say, "No Peter, it's too dangerous. You'll never make it." No, he believes in Peter! And he invites him to walk on the water in a storm. Now, it seems to me that this is not the ideal time to learn water-walking. Wouldn't it be much easier to practice on calm seas first? In truth, it probably would be. But perhaps the greatest miracles God works in our lives come during the worst times.

Most of you probably know the story from here. Peter gets out of the boat and walks on the water—for a little bit, anyway.

Matthew 14:30 records, "But when he saw the wind, he was afraid and, beginning to sink, cried out, 'Lord, save me!'" But Jesus was not offended by his childlike faith. I love the next verse. "Immediately Jesus reached out his hand and caught him" (v. 31). Jesus doesn't let him drown, nor does he reprimand Peter for being human.

But Jesus does ask an interesting question. "'You of little faith,' he said, 'why did you doubt?'" (v. 31). It's almost like he said, "With your faith, we could have walked all the way to the other side together. There's no reason to doubt, no matter how bad the storm is."

What exactly do you think Peter doubted? Did he doubt Jesus? I don't think so. When he started to sink, he immediately cried out to the Lord. He had faith in Jesus. He believed Jesus would rescue him.

So what did he doubt? He doubted himself! *I can't do this. The storm is too big. People can't walk on water. What was I thinking?*

I think God believes in us more than we believe in ourselves, I really do. The truth is, if we have faith in God, we can do everything that Jesus did—and more. Jesus said so himself in John 14:12. "I tell you the truth, anyone who has faith in me will do what I have been doing. He will do even greater things than these." I find that hard to believe, don't you? But anytime that Jesus starts a sentence with, "I tell you the truth," it's not because anything else he has said isn't true. It's because what he is about to say will be very hard for you and me to believe.

I have had times in my life when the storm was raging so hard that I simply wanted to give up and sink into my own grief and despair. I have thought many times, *I can't do this anymore! I'm not strong enough. Dying right now would be a relief.*

And on my own, that's true. I can't do it. But with even a little faith in Jesus, I can make it. I can walk on water.

Look how this storm story ends. "And when they climbed into the boat, the wind died down. Then those who were in the boat worshiped him" (vv. 32–33).

Once Jesus steps into the boat with them, the wind dies down and the storm subsides. The sea is calm once more. What is the disciples' response? They worship! This is certainly the appropriate response when God brings an end to the storm. It's right and good to worship God when he joins us in our own boat and calms the storm.

But I need to say this: it can be easy to worship God when the storm ends and things are good again, and when the storm isn't too fierce and doesn't last too long. It's easy to worship God when he answers our prayers with a yes. It's easy to worship God when he acts right, when he does what we ask for, when he makes our life better.

But what do you do when things don't get better? What do you do when the storm doesn't end? Or even worse, when the storm ends in tragedy? When the job loss effectively ends a career and leads to personal bankruptcy? When the illness ends in death? When a loved one gets cancer, goes through unbelievably painful treatments, and then dies anyway? How do you respond when you lose a son or a daughter in a car accident with a drunk driver?

What do you do when God doesn't act the way you think he should? Let's take it up a notch: What would you do if you knew that God was actually the cause of your storm?

Let me introduce you to a guy named Job.

Your Story

There's a temptation to think that only bad decisions lead to trouble. But several times Jesus led his disciples into storms.

Have you experienced a time when you thought you were being led by God into something, but it didn't go so well?

One definition for the word *grace* is "gift." How can this change your perspective on God and suffering?

Have you ever watched someone else go through a difficulty and said, "I could never do that"? Do you suppose that's what the eleven other disciples in the boat were saying about Peter?

Where is the grace of God inviting you to walk on the water with Jesus?

6

Six Words

"Have you considered my servant Job?" Six words. Who would've thought that six words could absolutely ruin someone's life? I mean, how devastating can six words be? It depends on who is speaking.

One of the most disturbing stories in all of Scripture is also one of the oldest, the story of a man named Job. Job likely lived in the second millennium BC, somewhere between the times of Abraham and Samson. And in one of the most ancient stories in the Bible, God provides us with an unsettling answer to the problem of human pain and suffering.

This is one of the few places in all of Scripture where God pulls back the curtain and lets us see exactly what is going on, both in heaven and on earth.

I kind of wish he didn't.

How God works in Job's story is not what I expected, and seeing it didn't give me the answers I was looking for. If anything, it just created more questions. If you're seeking answers to why bad things happen to good people, the book of Job provides an answer—in Technicolor! But it's probably not the answer you're expecting either.

Which brings me to the least obvious reason that storms come into our lives. What if a storm comes but it's not because you or anyone else is doing something wrong? What if a storm comes because you are doing something *right*?

Here's a little biblical theology you may not have heard before: bad things happen to good people precisely because they are good.

> *Bad things happen to good people precisely because they are good.*

Because they are doing things right. Because they are choosing good over evil. Because they are living by God's standards.

God's actions seem entirely counterintuitive. Our temptation when something really bad happens is to wonder what we did wrong. But sometimes bad things happen to us precisely because we're doing the right thing. This is Job's story.

But that's not all. Remember, I said the book of Job provides answers you may not like. And some answers actually create more questions.

Take a guess at who initiates the storm in Job's life.

Yep. God.

I call it "The Divine Setup."

A little background: Job was an all-around good guy, one of the wealthiest men of his time, with lots of servants and a diverse investment portfolio. His holdings included cattle, donkeys, sheep, and camels, numbering well into the thousands. Well-respected in his community, Job was known for his honesty and integrity. His pride and joy? Ten beautiful children: seven sons and three daughters.

In short, he had a good life. A really good life.

But not a perfect life.

Here's how the story unfolds.

> One day the angels came to present themselves before the
> LORD, and Satan also came with them. The LORD said to Satan,
> "Where have you come from?" Satan answered the LORD, "From
> roaming through the earth and going back and forth in it."
> (Job 1:6–7)

So far, so good. A little weird, maybe. I don't typically imagine God engaging in small talk with Satan. For that matter, what was Satan doing hanging around with the angels?

But I digress. Take a look at verse 8: "Then the LORD said to Satan, 'Have you considered my servant Job? There is no one on earth like him; he is blameless and upright, a man who fears God and shuns evil.'"

How about that? God is bragging on one of his children, to Satan of all things. And he notes, for public record, that Job is a good guy. In fact, there was no one quite like him on planet Earth: a man of integrity who loved and obeyed God and avoided sin. In short, Job did good things—all the time.

Now I always thought I'd like to hear God bragging on me. At least until I read this story. I would never have thought doing things right could end up causing so much trouble. Here's Satan's response:

> "Does Job fear God for nothing?" Satan replied. "Have you not
> put a hedge around him and his household and everything he
> has? You have blessed the work of his hands, so that his flocks
> and herds are spread throughout the land. But stretch out your
> hand and strike everything he has, and he will surely curse you
> to your face." (vv. 9–11)

As we like to say in the South, "Them's fightin' words!"

Satan basically blasts Job . . . and God. In essence, he said, "It's easy to trust God when things are going well. But you take away his prosperity and his household, and watch what happens. He will walk away from you so fast your head will spin!"

To which God responds, "Absolutely not! Job is a faithful servant of mine, and I will protect him, his family, and all that he has." Right?

Not so much.

God basically said, "Okay, have at him!"

Which brings me to another not so obvious reason really bad things happen to good people: God believes in you!

Check this out. God bet the farm on Job because he believed in him. Satan said Job's obedience was a sham. He only trusted God because his life was good. Satan argued to God that if he took away all Job's "blessings," Job would curse God to his face.

But God knew better. He believed in Job. And so he let Satan wreak havoc in his life to prove him wrong—and to perfect Job.

In the same way, God believes in you and me! When bad things come our way, God believes in us and knows that his strength is made perfect in our weakness. God is allowing us to be tested. Our lives are on display on earth and in heaven, and God expects us to prove him right—and Satan wrong.

God is preparing us for greatness. As a result, he's far more intent on perfecting us through storms than on protecting us from storms. And we will prevail.

God believes in us!

This isn't just Old Testament stuff either. Consider the life of the apostle Peter. From the time Peter dropped his nets and followed Jesus, God was intent on perfecting him through trials. In Luke 22:31–32, Jesus said, "Simon, Simon, Satan has asked to sift you as wheat. But I have prayed for you, Simon, that your faith may not fail. And when you have turned back, strengthen your brothers."

Several points of interest here. Number one, Satan asked for permission—again reminding us who is really in control of the situation. Then Jesus said he prayed for Peter. How cool is that? Jesus prays for us! Why? Because he believes in us. Look at what Jesus said next: "When you have turned back, strengthen your brothers." Jesus spoke prophetically about Peter's struggle and his eventual victory. He believed in him! He knew Peter would get through this. And on the other side, he would use this experience in Peter's life to strengthen other believers going through similar times of testing.

And that's exactly what happened. Remember Peter's words from 1 Peter 5:9–10?

> You know that your brothers throughout the world are undergoing the same kind of sufferings. And the God of all grace, who called you to his eternal glory in Christ, after you have suffered a little while, will himself restore you and make you strong, firm and steadfast.

Peter struggled through a severe trial of his faith, even denying any affiliation with Jesus for a brief period. But after he "suffered a little while," Jesus perfected him. Strong, firm, steadfast.

Like a rock.

Jesus actually prophesied this about Peter in John 1:42, years before it came to be. He said that Peter was presently known as Simon, son of John, but a day was coming when he would be known as Peter, which means *rock*. Pretty great, huh?

God believes in us more than we can imagine, and he is willing to put his reputation on the line because of his faith in us!

That's a little disquieting, isn't it? Might even fiddle with our theology a little, this idea that God has faith in us. But it's true.

God destined Peter for greatness. He destines us for greatness. Job too.

> The LORD said to Satan, "Very well, then, everything he has is in your hands, but on the man himself do not lay a finger." Then Satan went out from the presence of the LORD. (Job 1:12)

And so it begins.

Your Story

Job's story gives us a glimpse into what is happening in heaven when trouble comes. Have you ever thought about what the narrative of your story would look like if told from heaven's perspective?

Do you find the idea that Satan asked God for permission before he brought suffering into the lives of Job and Peter appalling or comforting?

Who was in control of Job's destiny in the story? Job? Satan? God?

Is it possible that God believes in you more than you believe in yourself?

PART 2

Your Worst Nightmare

What I feared has come upon me;

what I dreaded has happened to me.

— JOB 3:35 —

7

When God
Doesn't Act Right

Two roads diverged in a wood, and I—
I took the one less traveled by,
And that has made all the difference.

Robert Frost

Don't let the chapter title throw you. At an intellectual level, most of us would agree that God always does what's right. The problem comes when God doesn't do what we expect him to do or what *we* think is right.

I said earlier that it's easy to worship God when things are going well. But what do you do when things are going bad? Really bad? A single storm is one thing, but a perfect storm is a whole different animal. It's the collision of multiple storms at the same time. It's the moment where things go from bad to worse—and then worse again. Where one storm leads to another storm, and another, each one compounding the pain caused by the previous one. And there's no relief from any of them!

It's your worst nightmare. And there's no waking up.

Ultimately, I believe there are only two ways we can respond to God when we come face-to-face with our worst nightmare. Two paths we can take:

One less traveled by, and much more difficult.

The path of least resistance, well-worn by the feet of the majority.

A high road and a low road.

I know what you're thinking. *This guy is being way too simplistic. There are hundreds of different responses to God when tragedy strikes.* And that's true, to a degree. But ultimately people end up going in one of two directions, either consciously or unconsciously.

Now, the decision about which path to take is not always immediate, but it is inevitable. I have experienced enough trouble in my own life, and I've had enough conversations with people in crisis to know that a certain amount of time generally transpires before we are faced with this decision.

But we will face it.

Here's what I mean: when we experience a tragedy, there are two phases we often go through before we get to this tipping point. At first there's a "mind surge" phase where you are trying to get a grip on what just happened. It's like the adrenaline rush experienced when your physical body experiences trauma. The "what," "how," and "what next" questions are tumbling around inside your head like clothes in a dryer. For a short period of time, your intellect takes over so you can simply function. You do what has to be done. It's a little bit like when your computer crashes and reboots in "safe mode." You can perform basic duties, but no complex commands.

I've seen people at funerals in this "safe mode." Living from their intellect—surviving, really—they smile and shake hands and agree that their loved one is in a better place, that God is good, and they will be fine. They keep this up for the two to three days necessary to get through the visitation, funeral, and perhaps a graveside service. But like a physical adrenaline rush, it's short-lived. At some point, they crash.

The realization of what is lost and the uncertainty of what the future holds become more than the mind can process. Once the intellect is overwhelmed by the more powerful force of emotional pain, the mind and body go into shock. And with them, the soul.

This is the numbness stage.

In this second stage we don't really feel anything, much like physical shock. We might be dying because of a severed limb, but we can't feel it. Emotionally it's a form of self-protection. The pain is simply too great to bear, so we shut everything down.

I have seen mothers burying their children who were already at this stage. Eyes hollow and lifeless, they are semiaware of the people around them but make little or no effort to interact. They can't be comforted. To talk with anyone about their loss creates such an intense flood of emotions it threatens their sanity. So they feel nothing.

For a while.

The numbness stage can last for days, months, or even years. There is a part of us that would like to stay there for as long as we can. It seems better to feel nothing at all than to feel the deep pain we know is waiting. Or the violent anger, even rage, that's boiling just below the surface.

But eventually—after the adrenaline rush ends and the numbness fades away—we are faced with a decision about God.

At some point in our personal storm, we all have to come

to grips with what we really believe about God and suffering. And that journey will inevitably lead us down one of two paths.

We'll either choose to worship God . . . or to walk away from God.

Our unanswered questions, our emotional pain, and our inability to retrieve what was lost will take us down one of these paths. We'll either take a step toward God by faith, or step away from him.

We'll either choose to worship God . . . or to walk away from God.

Please don't misunderstand me. When I say walk away, I don't mean it's always a conscious, deliberate shaking of our fist at God like Lieutenant Dan in the storm in *Forrest Gump*. No, for most of us, it's more of a drift—almost unconscious, but not quite. We might still go to church, or read our Bible occasionally, but prayer sort of trails off. Or stops completely.

There's a dark part of us that feels somehow vindicated for giving up on God. Who could blame us?

But know this: it is a choice.

Both of these paths are graphically illustrated by two main characters in the story of Job. You remember him. Good guy, wealthy, with booming business and ten children he adored. More important though, he was a righteous man, a man who lived right. God himself said so.

You might also remember the little wager between God and Satan. Satan said Job only trusted God because God protected him and made his life comfortable. So God removed his protection and told Satan to have his way. There was only one caveat: "But on the man himself do not lay a finger" (Job 1:12).

To say that Satan has a field day would be an understatement.

Let me give you a quick recap of what happens in Job 1:13–17:

- In a hostile takeover by the Sabeans, Job loses all fifteen hundred of his cattle and donkeys, and all his servants in charge of them are killed.
- A freak firestorm wipes out all seven thousand of his sheep and the shepherds who tend them.
- Three Chaldean raiding parties swoop down on his camel farm, kidnap all his camels, and kill all his servants.

In a single day, Job loses all of his wealth, his business enterprises, and his earning potential. You have to remember this was long before the days of business or property insurance. He now stands bankrupt, with no source of income and no way to get any of it back. Job's situation is bad. Really bad.

But the sun hasn't set on Job's day. The proverbial "phone call" comes next.

> While he was still speaking, yet another messenger came and said, "Your sons and daughters were feasting and drinking wine at the oldest brother's house, when suddenly a mighty wind swept in from the desert and struck the four corners of the house. It collapsed on them and they are dead, and I am the only one who has escaped to tell you!" (Job 1:18–19)

I can't imagine the horror Job must feel. Everything else pales in comparison. Your children are having a family get-together at your oldest son's house and a tornado rips through the neighborhood and kills them. All of them.

All ten children. Gone. Forever.

Talk about the perfect storm. Job loses everything precious to him in a single twenty-four-hour period. It's his worst nightmare: "What I feared has come upon me; what I dreaded has happened to me" (3:25).

I can't fathom that kind of loss. I can't even begin to imagine the kind of pain, the kind of despair this would produce in the human soul. Losing your job or your financial well-being is one thing. Depressing, certainly. But losing your children? This is a whole different kind of pain. Deeper, more desperate. I know from personal experience that losing even one child is devastating. (I'll talk more about that later.) But to lose all of them? In one moment? There is really no word to describe Job's emotional state. Except maybe . . . suicidal. It's the most fitting word that comes to mind.

And angry. Violently angry. Talk about God not acting right.

Put yourself in Job's position for a minute. How would you feel? Better yet, what might you do?

Job is at the crossroads of faith and despair. And he makes a decision.

Your Story

Realizing that God allowed Satan to bring such devastation into Job's life, how does this make you *feel* about God?

Does it challenge what you have always believed about God?

In your own experience with suffering, what phase best describes where you are now: mind surge, numbness, or at the crossroads with God?

Has your pain brought you closer to God, or driven you further from God?

8

You've Got to Be Kidding!

> The LORD gave and the LORD has taken away;
> may the name of the LORD be praised.
>
> Job 1:21

So what was Job's response to the devastation in his life, his perfect storm?

> At this, Job got up and tore his robe and shaved his head. Then
> he fell to the ground in worship and said:
> "Naked I came from my mother's womb,
>   and naked I will depart.
> The LORD gave and the LORD has taken away;
>   may the name of the LORD be praised." (Job 1:20–21)

You've got to be kidding me. Praise God? Is Job completely out of touch with reality? He just lost ten children, for heaven's sake . . . literally! Honestly, this sounds like the kind of spiritual mumbo-jumbo I'd expect to hear from some televangelist trying to convince me I could earn God's favor by saying the "right thing" (and, of course, sending a generous donation to the ministry).

At first glance, I can't help but wonder if Job is in denial or something. But he isn't denying his pain. He recognizes his loss. He's in deep distress and everyone knows it. Note the shaved head and torn clothes. In the ensuing chapters, Job makes it very clear that his circumstances are extremely disagreeable to him, that he wishes he'd never been born.

But he makes a decision. In the wake of unbelievable loss, he chooses to worship.

Here's why I say it's a decision. It's easy to worship God when he does things I like—when things are going well, the blessings are pouring in, and our prayers are answered yes, and when the storm has a happy ending and no one gets hurt. I don't really have to make a decision about worshiping God then. It comes naturally because I "feel good" about God.

Which brings me to an important point about worship. Worship is not primarily a *feeling* I have about God. When things are going well, it's easy to slip into a "worship by default" mode. I don't even have to think about it. I just feel good about God, so worship comes easy . . . and it's shallow. But if my worship is by default, dependent on how I *feel* about God in light of my circumstances, then it's really not worship at all. It's more of a reciprocal back-scratching. *Thanks, God. You scratched my back, now I'll scratch yours.*

But that's not worship.

Worship is by definition the lesser giving honor and praise to the greater. Worship is a choice that I make about the greatness and goodness of God, whether things are going well or badly. Whether he answers my prayer with a resounding yes or a sobering no. Whether I feel like it . . . or not. Worshiping God when things are really bad doesn't come by default.

It's a decision.

King David is faced with this decision during one of his "perfect storms." Sadly, it is a storm of his own making. The story is told in 2 Samuel 11–12. David sinned against God by committing adultery with Bathsheba and killing her husband. She becomes pregnant from the affair, so he takes her to be his wife and they have a son together. Like any good father, David falls in love with this child.

But as a direct consequence of David's sin, God said that the boy would not live, and overnight the child becomes deathly ill. David is heartbroken, and I think probably conscience-stricken. This is his fault. Scripture records that David pleads with God to spare his child. He doesn't eat food or sleep in his bed. Instead, he lies on the ground and prays night and day that God would heal his son. His officials try to convince him to get up off the floor and eat, but he refuses. You can sense his desperation. *Please, God. Don't take my son. This is my fault, not his. If anything, take me! Please, please answer my prayer.*

Worship is a choice that I make about the greatness and goodness of God, whether things are going well or badly.

But David's sincere prayers go unanswered; his pleading with God is to no avail. On the seventh day, his son dies.

The storm ends in death.

Think about how you would feel if you were in David's shoes. Can you imagine the bitterness that would begin to overtake you in a moment like this? The anger at yourself—and at God? God could've healed the child. God could've prevented this outcome. (For that matter, I suppose God could've prevented David from sinning in the first place.)

But what did David do? "Then David got up from the ground.

After he had washed, put on lotions and changed his clothes, he went into the house of the LORD and worshiped" (2 Sam. 12:20).

He worshiped.

In the midst of painful regrets and unanswered prayers, he worshiped God. Like Job, David chose the high road.

The high road is the path less traveled because it is the path of greater resistance. We have to make a deliberate decision to worship God even when our emotions are screaming at us to do otherwise.

Let's go a little deeper here. As hard as it is to worship God when we're suffering the consequences of doing the wrong thing, imagine how hard it is to worship God when we're suffering because of doing the right thing.

In Acts 16, two missionaries are faced with exactly this dilemma. Paul and Silas are on a mission trip, serving God and telling folks the good news about following Jesus. Scripture makes it abundantly clear that God is leading them on this little expedition. In fact, two different times, it says that the Holy Spirit specifically prevented them from going somewhere they had planned to go. On top of that, God gives them a clear vision directing them to a city in Macedonia called Philippi.

Unlike our boy Jonah, they are obedient. They do the right thing. And God shows up in a powerful way. People respond to the gospel and begin to turn to God in repentance and faith. Some are healed from long-standing spiritual and physical maladies. One little slave girl suffering from demon-possession is miraculously freed from her spiritual bondage.

Good stuff.

But not everyone is happy with the little girl's newfound freedom. Turns out, there are a few people in the city who were making a lot of money on this little girl's demon-induced psychic abilities. So they incite a mob and get the whole city in an uproar against Paul and Silas. Without a trial, they are arrested by the authorities, severely flogged, and thrown in prison. To ensure there's no escape, they're put in the deepest, darkest part of the prison, their hands in chains, their legs in stocks. And by the way, the stocks weren't simply for containment purposes. They were used for torture.

All this for being obedient to God and helping others.

Good times.

Quick reality check here: How would you and I feel in that position? Maybe a little ticked off. Discouraged, certainly. Probably depressed. And afraid.

Now Scripture doesn't tell us what they *felt*, but it does tell us what they did. Check this out: "About midnight Paul and Silas were praying and singing hymns to God, and the other prisoners were listening to them" (Acts 16:25).

Really? Are you serious?

Let's see if I've got this right: they're arrested, sentenced without a trial, severely beaten, thrown in prison, and facing possible torture and/or execution. And they're praying and singing praise to God loud enough for the entire prison population to hear?

I mean, I get the praying part. I would definitely be praying. Something along the lines of "God, get me out of here!" But singing? Probably not.

But maybe, just maybe, there's something to this whole notion of praising God when life goes bad. Maybe it changes some things, even if our circumstances don't change.

Number one, praise changes our attitude. We move from thinking *Woe is me* to *Great is God*. The more we reflect on the greatness of God, the more our perspective on the situation changes. We're reminded that God is with us and he's always up to something. We just can't see it yet.

Praise gives us the strength to endure. This is perhaps the great secret Paul refers to later in life. Many of us know the famous quotation of Paul, "I can do all things through him who gives me strength." But most of us don't know the context. In case you've heard otherwise, it doesn't have anything to do with sports.

It's in the context of contentment in suffering. And he wrote it from prison.

> I have learned to be content whatever the circumstances. I know what it is to be in need, and I know what it is to have plenty. I have learned the secret of being content in any and every situation, whether well fed or hungry, whether living in plenty or in want. I can do everything through him who gives me strength. (Phil. 4:11–13)

I can do everything through him who gives me strength. I can endure injustice, suffering, imprisonment, torture, and even death. I know a secret.

It's interesting to me that Paul wrote this to the church in Philippi, the very city where he was imprisoned all those years before. I wonder if he wasn't reflecting back on that crazy night of praising God when the hour was darkest.

When he learned the secret.

The secret to contentment even when things are bad: worship God.

But that's not the weirdest part of the story. Not to me, anyway. I believe praising God changed Paul's whole perspective on things, maybe even what he was praying for. Here's why I say that: Have you ever prayed for something and then God did it, and you said, "Thanks, but no thanks. We're good here"?

Well that's basically what happens next. While Paul and Silas are praying and singing praise to God, suddenly there's a massive earthquake that shakes the very foundations of the prison and all the cell doors swing open. Not only that, but the chains fall from their wrists and the stocks holding their feet disintegrate.

Everybody's free to go!

But Paul and Silas don't go anywhere. What? I'd be like, "We are so out of here!" But their perspective has changed. God is up to something bigger than just releasing them from prison (which he does later anyway). He's raising up a new missionary, one who will be far more effective at reaching the citizens of Philippi than a couple of outsiders.

A jailer. On the inside.

When the jailer sees that the security of the prison he's responsible for has been compromised, he takes his sword and is about to end his own life. At which point, Paul steps in and tells him not to do it, because everyone is present and accounted for.

By the way, I'm not sure what kept the rest of the inmates from running away. Maybe they wanted to meet the singers and find out why they were so dang happy about imprisonment!

To make a long story short, the jailer comes to faith in Christ and takes the prisoners over to his house for a quick medical leave. As Paul's and Silas's wounds are being treated, they share the gospel and the whole household is saved and baptized: family, servants, everyone. Remember, God is always up to something. In this case, it turns out God was up to something a little bigger than a jailbreak.

Eventually Paul and Silas are released and head for a new town. But they are forever changed. They've learned the secret. The secret of being content in any circumstance. A secret only learned through trial and suffering and loss.

This is one of the main reasons I believe God doesn't protect us from suffering. There is something about suffering that deepens the soul. Something that takes our faith from the relative safety of the shallow end of the pool to the uncharted waters of the deep where it can grow. A place where our faith goes from believing in God to actually trusting God.

At some point in our lives, we'll all have to take that kind of journey. And while it's different for every person, it's also essentially the same. God is far more intent on perfecting our faith through trouble than on protecting us from trouble. He is not content for our faith to stagnate, for it to be stunted by the shallowness that often accompanies health, wealth, and prosperity. So he takes us on a journey.

To the deep end.

To a place where our feet can no longer touch the bottom. Where we are finally at the end of ourselves: the end of our strength, the end of our abilities, the end of what we can do, the end of our faith.

For my wife and me, it was the day we lost our only daughter.

Your Story

Has your worship of God been a deliberate decision or more of a default based on circumstances or feelings?

Have you ever thought about the "secret of contentment in every circumstance" being worship and praise?

How would you describe your attitude when things are hard?

Take time to praise God right now no matter what your circumstances.

9

Going Off the Deep End

I told you a little of my family's story earlier, but let me fill in some of the details. It was the culmination of the worst three years of our lives, a true perfect storm. I had resigned the church where I had pastored for seven years and moved my family to Denver to plant a new church with no money, no sponsors, and no job. I had been without a paycheck in Huntsville for about eleven months and now we were living off credit cards in Denver. I prayed and prayed for God to provide for us financially, but it never happened. We just got further and further behind. We were at the end of our rope financially, over $70,000 in debt, with no relief in sight.

Emotionally, my wife and I were just shot. We were both suffering from severe depression, but my wife's emotional state was getting desperate. The pain of leaving the church where we had built so many life-giving relationships, compounded by the fact that we were now twelve hundred miles away from family and friends, was killing her. Add to that the emotional strain of our ever-worsening financial situation, and she was at the end of her rope. Outwardly I was trying to stay positive, saying things like, "Hang in there. God's going to help us. We just need to trust him."

But inwardly, I was beginning to wonder.

While all this was going on, we found out about a young lady we'll call Sonya, who was pregnant and considering whether or not to keep the child. A friend of a friend gave us her number and asked if we would consider talking to her about possibly adopting her child. She lived in Denver, so I called and set up an appointment to meet with her. We had a great conversation that day and she made the decision to let us adopt her child.

To qualify for any type of adoption, you've got to be gainfully employed and prove that you can actually provide for a child. I had to get a job and fast. Since the church-planting thing wasn't working out, we moved back to Huntsville where I took a sales job with a printing company. I had just enough room on one last credit card to come up with a deposit and the first month's rent on a small house in the area. We were maxed out on credit now, but I felt like we were finally getting a chance to start over.

I was relieved to be out of a ministry position and back in the marketplace I had left years earlier to become a pastor. I knew the printing industry pretty well and felt it would only be a matter of time before I was making six figures. We could pay it all off in time. I began to feel some hope.

The excitement of this fresh start was increased by the prospect of adding another child to our family. We had one four-year-old son already and he'd been asking about a brother or sister for a while now. It looked like he was finally going to get his wish! My wife Marlina was coming alive again, back in her home state, enjoying the renewed proximity to her girlfriends and family. She was setting up a nursery for the new baby, preparing her son for preschool, and starting to feel normal again. I had a new job, we were in a new house, and we were only weeks away from having a new baby.

Problem was, I was still depressed. I had a lot of unanswered questions in my heart about the struggles in Denver. *Where was God in all of this? Was God in any of it? Why didn't he help us?* We were trying to do the right thing, trying to help people, sharing the good news. But it was as if God was nowhere to be found. I didn't talk to anyone about my disillusionment. I had always thought that people who whined about God "not coming through" were just emotionally unstable or spiritually immature, or some combination of both.

Kind of like me.

But there was still a bright spot in our lives. A ray of hope in an otherwise dismal forecast.

Zoe Marie.

Just after I had taken my new job, our baby girl was born. However, it came as a surprise to us. Up to this time, we'd been in weekly contact with Sonya, who now lived in Huntsville. Strangely enough, even though she had lived in Denver when we met, her parents lived in Huntsville and she decided to move back in with them during her pregnancy. But in the past few weeks, she had broken contact with us. We got word through our lawyer in Birmingham that she had delivered the baby. As we picked him up from the airport, he filled us in on the situation. Sonya was having second thoughts, but still wanted to go through with the adoption. He thought she was committed to the adoption, but believed she just needed a little more time to process the decision.

Then he posed a question. A question I've had a lot of "if onlys" about ever since. He asked if we were willing to take home a "conflicted child," meaning that the mother had not yet surrendered her parental rights. In other words, worst-case scenario, she could take the baby back at some point.

I immediately said no. I mean, who wants to open their heart to that kind of potential disaster?

Apparently my wife did.

Without any hesitation, even after hearing my response, she said, "Absolutely yes!" She knew the first few weeks were a critical time for bonding with a new child and she wasn't going to jeopardize that window of opportunity. She knew the risks and was willing to take them. I sensed immediately this was not an argument I was going to win.

We brought our little girl home.

Marlina immediately jumped in and did the things only a mom can do. She quickly settled Zoe into a comfortable rhythm of feeding, changing, playing, and napping. She gave her whole heart to that child from day one, never hesitating. She knew in her heart that this was her daughter. The light was back in her eyes, and I was enjoying seeing her genuinely happy again.

My son Zachary loved having a little sister. He would play with her for hours on end, even when she was supposed to be napping. He would inundate her little world with his collection of stuffed animals. He would place them in a circle around her and then bring each one close to her face, telling her its name and its place in his world. He especially loved to hold her for her last feeding before she went to bed for the night. He was a great big brother.

I did everything I could not to fall in love with that child.

It didn't work.

After several weeks of fighting for the safety of my own heart, I finally yielded to the little bright-eyed beauty. She simply stole my heart. I was her Daddy and she was Daddy's girl. I wasn't enjoying my job at the printing company very much, but knowing I would come home to those sparkling eyes helped me make it through the day.

By the way, have you ever tried to succeed in a sales job when you're depressed? In the old days, I was the guy who could sell ice to an Eskimo. Now I couldn't sell candy to a preschooler. Seriously. It was a disaster. In the first month, I only sold a few business cards. The next two months weren't much better. About ninety days in, I knew they were going to have to fire me. I mean, if I was the boss, I would fire me. In all fairness, there were some internal problems at the company as well. The few jobs I did sell were done poorly, delivered late, and overbilled. Not a good combination. So I did everyone a favor and resigned.

Still, as bad as things were on the career and financial front, our family was doing better than ever.

We named our daughter Zoe because that's the Greek word translated *life*. Not physical, breathing life; that's the word *bios*. No, *zoe* means the inner life, a deeper life, the kind of life Jesus was talking about when he said that he came "that we might have life to the full."

Turns out, she lived up to her name. Because the deeper life only comes from a journey to the deep end.

It was a few days before Christmas and we were busily preparing for a road trip to visit my family in Tennessee. Marlina couldn't wait to show off her new daughter and was excited about all the new clothes, toys, and assorted baby items she knew were coming at Christmas. Even though my work situation was entirely uncertain, I experienced a weird kind of joy every time I held my little girl. We would get through this. Our whole family would. Together.

When the phone call came from Sonya, our world went into a bizarre kind of slow motion. She wanted to come get her baby right away, but we asked if we could keep her until Christmas Eve. Then we would bring Zoe to her. We didn't want our son to see her being taken from us, but given by us. We spent the next three days memorizing every moment with Zoe Marie. Even the simplest things became sacred. Every feeding, every nap, every changing, every bath was accompanied by tears, an emotional combination of joy and sorrow.

Giving up our child was a painfully slow process. Even though we brought Zoe to Sonya on Christmas Eve, she insisted that she hadn't decided for sure; she just needed to be with the child to make that kind of decision. In retrospect, I think she was trying to let us down easy, but in reality, it just made it harder on us. We didn't know whether to grieve or to hope.

Frankly, I was going numb to the whole thing. I hardened my heart and made every effort not to care. Somehow, men are able to do this. But my wife was in a fragile state and I worried for her.

We would visit Zoe at her grandparents' house about once a week. Each time we visited, I knew that we needed to get some closure on this, or my wife was going to go over the edge. But any time I brought up the subject of insisting on a decision, Marlina would plead with me to give her one more week, clinging to the slim hope that Sonya still might make the decision for adoption.

After several weeks of this bizarre visitation ritual, I told Marlina I couldn't go back anymore. I was done. This created a whole new tension between Marlina and me, but now I felt like I was the one who was going to go over the proverbial "cliffs of insanity." If I had to venture into that house one more time and see my daughter in someone else's family, I was going to scream. But Marlina wanted me to hang on, thinking that my absence would signal a lack of concern to Sonya. For a husband, it was a dreaded "no-win" situation.

So we held on for a bit longer.

But after several more weeks of the waiting game, Marlina and I finally sat down with Sonya and told her we had to have a decision. It wasn't fair to anybody to go on like this: not to her, not to us, and certainly not to Zoe. It was the prompting she needed to verbalize the decision that her heart had made months before. She would keep the baby.

It was over.

It's sometimes hard for my wife and me to explain to others what we mean when we say "We lost our daughter." She didn't die. She wasn't kidnapped. I can't say that I totally know the pain a parent feels when going through either of those scenarios. But there is a deep pain that a parent experiences when they know their child is alive and well but separated from them forever. They still love that child deeply, but can't be with them. For me this was compounded by the fact that this child would not have a father, and every daughter deserves to have a loving father.

Marlina and I learned through counseling that it does no good to try and compare our suffering to the suffering of others. The bottom line is that loss is loss, and pain is pain.

It's what we do in response to suffering that matters.

I'll never forget the night when we said our final good-byes to Zoe Marie as our daughter. As we left the house where she would stay now, the sadness was overwhelming. Marlina was sobbing and couldn't be comforted. I was trying to be strong, but it was everything I could do just to drive home. We got home and put our son to bed in silence. There's a certain silence that is only brought on by loss, the kind of silence you experience at a funeral. It's a mixture of not having anything to say, despair so strong it feels like it will suffocate you, and the fear that if you say anything you'll lose control and never get it back. And in the silence of that dark night, my wife and I made a decision.

To worship.

We put a collection of worship CDs into our stereo, cranked up the volume, sat down on our couch, and listened. We held each other tightly as our bodies trembled and we began to sob.

We cried like we've never cried before or since. We never sang a word, but we worshiped.

And in those few hours together on the couch, God came to us.

He comforted us, but it wasn't the kind of comfort that takes away the pain. The pain was still excruciating. We were comforted simply by his presence, by the reality that he loved us deeply and was joining us in our pain. He was not distant, unaware, or unaffected. He bore it with us.

We learned the ancient secret that night. The secret of finding peace and contentment no matter what the circumstance. The power of worship.

We still felt overwhelming sorrow. But on that night, we could say along with Job, "He gives and takes away. Blessed be the name of the Lord."

Your Story

Have you ever found yourself saying the "right" things about God to others, but not really believing them yourself?

Have you experienced a ray of hope in the midst of suffering only to have it dashed later?

Have you been tempted to compare your suffering to others? Maybe sought to minimize your own pain because it's not as "bad" as someone else's? Or allowed bitterness to creep in because it seems worse than others' pain?

Have you ever deliberately worshiped God in the midst of great pain or loss? Describe what you felt in that moment.

10

It Is Well with My Soul

There's an old, well-known hymn that was birthed through the painful decision to worship God in the midst of loss. Horatio Gates Spafford, the author of this hymn, was a nineteenth-century Job. Many people have heard his story over the years, but many don't know the story behind the story, the story from the Bible that provoked not only the title but the primary theme as well.

It's an obscure Old Testament story found in 2 Kings 4. There's a woman living in a town called Shunem whose husband is up in years, and they're childless. The prophet Elisha travels through this town frequently, but apparently has no place to stay. So she and her husband build an upper room for him to use when he's in town. Elisha wants to thank the couple for their hospitality, but they don't ask for anything. However, when Elisha finds out that they are childless, he makes a bold promise to the woman that she'll bear a son within the year.

Sure enough, a year later she has a son who becomes a delight to his parents. One day, while he's still very young, he asks his dad if he can go work in the fields with him. Dad gives him the okay, but as the morning wears on, the son gets a bad headache, perhaps a little heat stroke. Apparently not too worried, Dad sends him back to the house to stay with Mom until he feels better. The son sits on her lap until noon, then dies suddenly. Scripture tells us that after laying the lifeless body of her son in Elisha's room, she's very distressed, and sets out on a mission to find Elisha.

When Elisha sees her coming, he sends his servant to ask her how she and her husband are doing and specifically asks about her son.

Check out her response. "And she answered, '*It is* well'" (2 Kings 4:26 NKJV).

Pardon me? *It is well?* I would expect something radically different from a woman whose only son has just died unexpectedly. More like, "It is not good. Not good at all." Or maybe the Hebrew equivalent of, "Life stinks right now!" The word translated "well" is the Hebrew word *shalom*, which means happy or prosperous; contented; at peace. In the midst of her obvious distress, she is able to say, "I am at peace." Content.

Fast-forward to the end of the story. Elisha comes to her home and God miraculously raises her son back to life. Pretty amazing stuff. But what amazes me most is the steady, unwavering faith she demonstrated in saying, "It is well," while her son lay dead in an upper room, *before* he was miraculously raised from the dead.

This startling confession of faith *before a resurrection* provides the backdrop and serves as the inspiration for Horatio Spafford's similar confession in 1873.

Now to his family's story.

In the 1860s Horatio and Anna Spafford enjoyed the perfect life in many ways. Horatio was a prominent lawyer and successful businessman in Chicago, and good friends with noted evangelist D. L. Moody. They had four beautiful children, all daughters. In addition to his successful law practice, Horatio had a number of real estate holdings in Chicago, making them a very wealthy family indeed.

In addition to all of these business pursuits, they participated actively in the work of their local church. Horatio was an elder and Sunday school teacher. He particularly enjoyed teaching children. Above and beyond their church work, they were heavily involved in philanthropic work in Chicago, including the abolitionist crusade to end slavery.

They were poster children for the victorious Christian life.

Their perfect storm began in 1871. That was the year of the Great Chicago Fire that destroyed almost four square miles of downtown Chicago, including all of Spafford's real estate investments. He literally watched them go up in smoke. The only real estate left was their house, which was spared because it was on the north side of town.

The fire was one of the most catastrophic disasters of the nineteenth century. Hundreds of lives were lost, seventeen thousand buildings were destroyed, and thousands upon thousands of people were left homeless. The city was crippled. But instead of fleeing the city, the Spaffords used what resources they had left to reach out to the displaced residents of Chicago, now refugees in their own city. The Spaffords fed the hungry, assisted the homeless and poor, and in general helped folks get back on their feet again.

In the midst of their loss, they chose to help others. To do the right thing.

But the worst of the storm was still to come.

After two years of these relief efforts, Anna Spafford's health began to decline, and upon doctors' orders Horatio decided to take his family on a much-needed vacation in Europe. The plan was to eventually meet up with D. L. Moody, who was conducting an evangelistic campaign in Great Britain.

He traveled with his wife and four daughters to New York City, where they were all to board the French vessel *Ville de Havre* for their trip to Europe. At the last minute, Horatio was detained by a business obligation. A prospective investor had died suddenly and Horatio would have to return to Chicago immediately. They made the decision for the family to go on ahead of him. He would join them shortly, as soon as his business affairs could be put in order.

At 2:00 a.m. on November 22, 1873, their ocean liner was rammed by a cargo vessel en route to Europe. The collision all but cut the *Ville de Havre* in half, and she sank into the icy depths of the North Atlantic in twelve minutes. Anna's last memory before she lost consciousness was of her two-year-old daughter being torn from her arms as she was violently sucked beneath the waves.

In all, 226 of the 307 passengers aboard the vessel died, including all four Spafford daughters. Anna survived and was picked up by crew members of the ship that had struck them, unconscious but clinging to a piece of floating debris. A fellow survivor of the disaster, Pastor Nathaniel Weiss, recalled Anna saying after their rescue, "God gave me four daughters. Now they have been taken from me. Someday I will understand why."

You can sense her disillusionment, her frustration with the questions that have no answers. She recognized her children were a gift from God. But now they were gone. Taken. Why? She didn't specifically say that God took them away, but you can sense her faith dilemma. *Why didn't God save them? He could have. Why?*

Upon reaching Cardiff, Wales, she wired her husband, "Saved alone. What shall I do?" In those few words, telegraphed to a husband thousands of miles away, the loneliness and despair she felt are evident. But I think there's more to it than that.

Saved alone.

A twinge of guilt. She survived. Her four daughters froze to death or drowned in the harsh North Atlantic Sea, but somehow she survived. She'd have gladly traded her life for theirs in a moment.

Why me and not them?

I can't even begin to imagine that kind of pain.

As soon as Horatio got the telegram, he boarded the first ship to Europe to join his grief-stricken wife. As a husband and father, I can only speculate about what he might have been thinking.

If only.

If only I had made the family wait and come back with me to Chicago.

If only I had gone ahead with them, I could have gotten them into a lifeboat.

If only that investor hadn't died.

If only God . . .

The possibilities in those three words are unlimited.

On the way across the Atlantic, in the midst of his own pain, I imagine him trying to think of any words that might be able to comfort to his wife—and finding none. Late one evening, he was told by the captain of the ship that they had reached the place of the fateful collision that stole his daughters from him. And as the ship passed over the very waters where the *Ville de Havre* rested some three miles below; where the bodies of his four daughters lay without the dignity of a burial, he penned these words:

> When peace, like a river, attendeth my way,
> When sorrows like sea billows roll;

Whatever my lot, Thou has taught me to say,
It is well, it is well, with my soul.

As he looked over the sea that had swallowed his children, he could see ocean swells rising and falling, then crashing against the ship. Swells that mirrored the wave after wave of emotional pain crashing against his heart.

Sorrows like sea billows.

Waves of sadness and despair that threatened to capsize his faith in God. But as he chose the path of worship in the time of his greatest loss, he was able to say, "It is well with my soul."

But that's not the end of their story. For Horatio and Anna Spafford, the storm wasn't over yet. In 1880, their beloved four-year-old son, their only son, died of scarlet fever.

They learned, as you and I will, that it can always get worse.

Your Story

How could any mother say, "It is well," when she's just lost her son? What does this tell you about her faith? Her hope in God?

Have you ever experienced a sense of guilt because you have been spared from a tragedy that others have had to endure?

Have you mentally gone through a series of "if onlys" in your suffering?

How would you describe your soul right now? Well? Not well? Conflicted?

11

It Can Always Get Worse

Yet when I hoped for good, evil came;
when I looked for light, then came
darkness.

Job 30:26

In my early years of pastoral counseling, I would always assure people that things were going to get better. I felt that those words would somehow ease the pain of their situation.

At least it made me feel better.

In fact, some people's situations were so awful, so tragic, that I honestly couldn't imagine anything worse. I assumed that things could only get better from here.

I don't say that anymore. Now I tell people going through trouble that it can always get worse. That may sound cynical, but we set ourselves up for even greater disappointment (and disillusionment) when we insist that God is going to fix everything, ideally soon.

I have a good friend, a young man with his whole life ahead of him, who went through a long ordeal with cancer. He found out about the cancer by accident. He was having a routine checkup at his eye doctor when the optometrist noticed that he could look left, right, and down just fine, but he couldn't look up as much as normal. Sure enough, they discovered a mass. Cancer. The bad kind, growing fast and usually a killer.

But he demonstrated an extraordinary trust in God, particularly for a teen. His attitude was upbeat and his disposition was cheerful. And after an unbelievable amount of radiation and chemotherapy that almost killed him, the doctors pronounced his cancer to be in a state of remission. No guarantees for how long, but he was good for now.

The storm was over.

However, his quality of life was forever altered. He walked with a distinct limp, the aftereffects of brutal radiation treatments, and the hair on his head would never grow back. The cancer treatments had also rendered him sterile. But he was determined to make the best of his situation.

So he married his girlfriend, who had stood by his side through the whole ordeal. I'll never forget the song they played at the wedding, "Here I Am to Worship." I was standing onstage that day, serving as one of his groomsmen, and I just lost it. It was such a beautiful picture of God's redemption and restoration. After the wedding, they moved into a house just down the road from his parents. They both got jobs in the community and began their new life together. Things were finally looking up.

But it can always get worse.

One day, as he was working around the house, he thought he smelled smoke. He walked outside and saw that his garage was on fire. Because it was a detached garage, his first thought was that their house wasn't in any danger. But before he even had time to dial 911, the combination of intense heat and high winds quickly spread the flames to the main house. He ran in to save what he could—some pictures, personal letters, and journals—but within minutes the entire house was an inferno. He watched helplessly as their new home burned to the ground, and with it all of their earthly belongings.

So much for a fresh start.

Someone offered to let the couple stay in their garage apartment until they could work out something permanent. Other folks generously donated food and clothes, but it was an incredibly difficult time. They both just wanted to run away and take a never-ending vacation.

But they hadn't lost everything. Two things survived the fire.

First, the aforementioned pictures, letters, and journals, which provided them with a link to their past. During the years of their courtship and his cancer journey, they had taken many pictures and had saved all the letters they had written back and forth. In addition, they had written extensively about their experiences and their walk with God in personal journals. It wasn't much, but it was something. Something tangible that proved their existence before the fire.

The other thing that survived the fire was several thousand dollars' worth of tools. He was a handyman by trade and his tools were the way he made his living. They could start over. Since there wasn't enough room in the garage apartment, they stored the surviving mementos and valuable tools in his parents' garage for safekeeping.

Not for long.

Several weeks later, a freak fire broke out at his parents' house. The house itself was spared, but you want to take a wild guess at what burned to the ground?

The garage.

With all their mementos and tools. The only things that had survived the first fire. Now, that's just wrong! I mean, how much can one couple take?

In the words of Bachman-Turner Overdrive, "You ain't seen nothing yet."

Let's pick up the story of Job where we left off: Job's lost almost everything, including his wealth, his livelihood, and all of his children. In Job's case, most people would have told him it couldn't get any worse.

But it can.

"Then the LORD said to Satan, 'Have you considered my servant Job?'" (Job 2:3).

No, please God. Not again. The last time you spoke those words I lost everything!

Well, not quite everything.

God continues, "There is no one on earth like him; he is blameless and upright, a man who fears God and shuns evil. And he still maintains his integrity, though you incited me against him to ruin him without any reason" (v. 3).

God argues to Satan that Job was and still is a righteous man, who hasn't lost his faith even though he's lost just about everything else. He also states that Job didn't do anything wrong to deserve this kind of suffering and takes personal responsibility for Job's "ruin."

In essence, he was telling the accuser, "You lose. You said that he would curse me to my face if anything ever happened to his family and his stuff. But you were wrong! His faith is as strong as ever, even though he's done nothing to deserve this."

Game over, right? God wins, Satan loses, and hopefully Job gets some semblance of a life back. Wrong. In what could be described as a cosmic poker game, Satan's back is against the wall, but he still has an ace up his sleeve. Job hasn't lost everything. Not yet.

It can always get worse.

There was one area of Job's life that God hadn't let Satan touch: his health. "On the man himself, do not lay a finger," remember? Apparently Satan was a firm believer that "if a man's got his health, he's got everything." So he plays his final card.

"Skin for skin!" Satan replied. "A man will give all he has for his own life. But stretch out your hand and strike his flesh and bones, and he will surely curse you to your face" (vv. 4–5).

To which, if I were writing the story, God would have replied, "No way! He's had enough already. In fact, this whole thing has got entirely out of hand. I can't believe I let you talk me into this in the first place. No more. We're done here."

Not exactly.

> The LORD said to Satan, "Very well, then, he is in your hands; but you must spare his life." [Ironically, this is the one thing that God spared that Job wished he had lost.] So Satan went out from the presence of the LORD and afflicted Job with painful sores from the soles of his feet to the top of his head. Then Job took a piece of broken pottery and scraped himself with it as he sat among the ashes. (vv. 6–8)

In round two of the aforementioned "bizarre competition," God now allows Satan to take away Job's health, afflicting him head to foot with painful boils. But it's much worse than just boils. As you read further in the book, Satan causes some kind of systemic disease that includes fever, insomnia, flesh-blackening gangrene, radical weight loss, and constant pain. Everything short of death. His body is so disfigured that when his friends show up in chapter 3, they don't even recognize him.

His wife is noticeably bummed.

Which leads us to the second path we can take when things go really bad.

Your Story

Have you already experienced the reality that "it can always get worse"? Talk about it.

On the other hand, knowing that things can always get worse is different than believing they will always get worse. Have you found yourself living in a state of foreboding, just "waiting for the other shoe to drop"?

Have you ever experienced a long-term illness and its subsequent effects on your emotional health?

What do you think Job's emotional state was at this point?

12

The Path
of Least Resistance

His wife said to him, "Are you still holding on
to your integrity? Curse God and die!"

Job 2:9

I love doing just about anything outdoors, but I have a particular
love for hiking and backpacking. I've logged over five hundred
miles on the Appalachian Trail, and in the last few years I've had
the opportunity to lead three groups of men to the summit of
the highest mountain in the continental United States, Mount
Whitney. At 14,500 feet, it's quite a climb, but the rush you feel
when you reach the top makes it all worth it.

Now, here's what you'll learn very quickly about hiking in the
mountains: it's a whole lot harder to go up than it is to go down.

When you're going up, gravity is working against you, resist-
ing your efforts to make forward progress. But going down is
much easier. Gravity is working for you, literally pulling you

down the mountain. As a result, on steep downgrades you have to work pretty hard to slow your descent enough to keep yourself from falling.

Emotional pain is a lot like gravity.

Remember I said there were basically two ways to respond to tragedy? The second option is what I call the low road. It's the path of least resistance. We simply walk away from God. The gravity of emotional pain pulls us down, taking us further and further away from God. It doesn't really demand making a deliberate decision. But like a mountain descent, the steeper the grade—the greater the emotional pain—the stronger the pull is away from God.

Meet Job's wife.

Now, we don't typically think of Job's wife as a main character in the story because so little is said about her. We focus almost solely on Job and his painful trial. If anything *is* said about her in a sermon, she is simply chided for her lack of faith in God, or even included as another one of Job's trials. You know—Job is going through all this stuff and now he's got to deal with her!

I don't know very much about her, but I'm pretty clear about how she felt about her life . . . and God. "Are you still holding on to your integrity? Curse God and die!" she said. The anger and pain and bitterness pour out of her mouth from the depths of her soul. "Really. Are you serious, Job? Do you still trust God after all of this? Do you still think God is all good and powerful now? Forget God. Just walk away. If he doesn't like it, he can just strike you dead."

Or me.

I'll grant you, that sounds pretty bad, but before we crucify her, let's walk a mile in her shoes. There's a temptation to define her by a single statement recorded in a moment of unbelievable pain.

Think about it. She lost the same stuff Job lost. All their wealth is gone and with it, her sense of financial stability and security. And now all of that's compounded by the fact that he can't work. But far more importantly, she also just lost all of her children. Put yourself in her position for just a minute. How would you feel if all of your children were killed in one day by a freak storm?

A storm God could have prevented.

I think we are a little too quick to judge her because of her lack of faith and trust in God.

But can you really blame her?

I can't.

I've found myself questioning the goodness of God in the face of far less painful losses. I can't throw any stones. I've wanted to give up on God myself.

When we're going through tremendous suffering and pain, there's a side of us that just wants to give up and "go off the deep end." *Who cares?*

I've been there.

In my journey through suffering, all sorts of temptations that were formerly manageable suddenly seemed irresistible. An affair with another woman, real or imagined, seemed reasonable, even fair. (I wonder if that's why it's called an "a fair." A chance to get even with a spouse, or even with God himself. Hmm.)

A dark side started manifesting itself that made me want to just forget about following God and do my own thing. Pursue pleasure. Use people. Ignore others. *It doesn't really matter. Either way you get pain.*

I remember the night we got the final word that the birthmother was going to keep Zoe. Our baby girl. My daughter. Weeks and months of pent-up frustration—frustration from constantly doing and saying the right things without getting the right results—just blew up inside me. I was suddenly enraged at the unfairness of it all. I remember storming out of the restaurant where my wife and I were eating, leaving her alone at the table. I jumped into my car, threw it in gear, and floored it, leaving black marks and smoke across the parking lot. I blasted across two lanes of traffic without looking, tires spinning wildly, not caring if I wrecked or got arrested.

Just try and pull me over right now.

I was racing down the road, thinking that if I could just find a bar, I'd pull in and get wasted. *Why not? It doesn't matter anyway.* Maybe even find a pretty little woman to get in some trouble with. You know, some short-term pleasure to help dull the pain.

To shake my fist at God. *Maybe he'll take me out.*

Did I mention that I'm a pastor?

This is one of many reasons I have so much respect for Job. Listen to what is recorded after he lost everything: "Not once through all this did Job sin. He said nothing against God" (Job 2:10 Message).

That's absolutely amazing to me. Not once in all of this—the loss of his wealth, the loss of his livelihood, the loss of his health, the loss of ten children, for heaven's sake—not once in all of this did he sin. Now it's important to note that Scripture doesn't say Job wasn't tempted to sin. It just says he didn't.

This Is a Test. This Is Only a Test.

Years ago, before the age of digital technology, there was a really bizarre thing that would happen while you were watching television. (Some cable systems still do a similar thing periodically.) You'd be watching one of your favorite shows, and all of a sudden the screen would go blank, then start showing multi-colored horizontal bars. You'd hear a series of annoying beeps, then a monotone voice would come on. "This is a test of the emergency broadcast system. This is only a test. If this were a real emergency, you would be notified of what to do." It only lasted maybe thirty seconds, but it seemed like an eternity. It inevitably came in the middle of the most pivotal point in the whole show. It always ticked me off.

Here's something I experienced going through my perfect storms: when life starts looking bad, sin starts looking good. There's a reason for that. Suffering is a test. It's also a temptation.

Same thing, in fact.

In Scripture, there is an interesting Greek word that is used synonymously but translated two different ways. It's the word *peirazo*. It means "to test," but it is often translated "to tempt." Same word, but translated two different ways. What's with that?

Some would say it points to a contradiction in Scripture.

One of the most alarming examples of this in Scripture is in relation to Jesus right after he was baptized by John the Baptist. The Gospel of Matthew records, "Then Jesus was led by the Spirit into the desert to be *tempted* by the devil" (Matt. 4:1, italics mine).

"Tempted." There's that word, *peirazo*.

What makes this story particularly bothersome is that Scripture states Jesus was being led by the Spirit to be tempted. Whoa now, wait just a minute! Doesn't the Bible teach that God doesn't tempt anyone? Scripture makes it clear in the book of James that God will never tempt us to do evil (see 1:13). So what's up?

Well, you have to remember, *peirazo* is also translated as "to be tested." All three of the Gospel accounts that speak of the "temptation of Christ" could just have easily been translated "the testing of Christ." So here's where I've landed on the whole thing: while God will never tempt us, he will most certainly test us. When Jesus was led by the Spirit into the wilderness, was it for a time of temptation . . . or testing?

Yes.

It's not an either-or. Both were happening at the same time, and it's the same for us today. When we're going through a time of testing, it's also a time of temptation.

If it's the same Greek word translated both ways, is there really a difference? In fact, there's a huge difference! The difference is this:

God uses testing as an opportunity for us to do good.

Satan uses tempting as an enticement for us to do wrong.

That's the reason sin can look so good when life looks so bad. Again, this is one of the reasons I believe God is far more intent on perfecting us through trouble than on protecting us from trouble. In adversity, we learn to overcome sin. Peter said it this way: "He who has suffered in his body is done with sin" (1 Pet. 4:1). There's something about suffering adversity, and suffering temptation, that teaches us to say no to sin.

This was true for Jesus. Many of us have an unrealistic view of Jesus in his time spent on earth, thinking that he never really had to endure temptation the way we do. But Scripture makes it very clear that Jesus "suffered" temptation. Hebrews 4:15 reminds us, "For we do not have a high priest who is unable to sympathize with our weaknesses, but we have one who has been tempted in every way, just as we are—yet was without sin." The writer of Hebrews goes on to say, "Although he was a son, he learned obedience from what he suffered and, once made perfect, he became the source of eternal salvation for all who obey him (Heb. 5:8–9). Jesus was made perfect through suffering. *Whoa!*

Wait just a minute! I thought Jesus was already perfect. And what's all that about learning obedience?

Here's the deal: Jesus was fully God and fully human on earth. But his perfection was proven by testing, by his obedience to the Father's will, and by his endurance through suffering.

The same goes for you and me.

I never liked tests. I still don't. But what I really hate are pop quizzes. Remember those? You know, you showed up on a Wednesday thinking that the school day was going to be a breeze. Then your teacher tells you to get out a sheet of paper and a no. 2 pencil.

There's something about suffering adversity, and suffering temptation, that teaches us to say no to sin.

Dang it! Pop quiz. *I really wish I'd taken some notes earlier.*

It's the same thing with life tests. They always come in the form of a pop quiz. No warning, no time to brush up on your memory verses. You're just suddenly smack in the middle of it. Makes you wish you'd been praying more, maybe.

Here's some good news! God didn't strike Job's wife dead for her emotional outbursts, and he hasn't struck me dead for my emotional outbursts either. God understands the human condition. Psalm 103 reminds us of the graciousness of God toward us in our human frailty.

> He does not treat us as our sins deserve
>   or repay us according to our iniquities.
> For as high as the heavens are above the earth,
>   so great is his love for those who fear him;
> as far as the east is from the west,
>   so far has he removed our transgressions from us.

> As a father has compassion on his children,
>> so the LORD has compassion on those who fear him;
> for he knows how we are formed,
>> he remembers that we are dust. (Ps. 103:10–14)

He remembers that we are dust.

I don't know about you, but I think that's beautiful. God understands the human condition. He knows how weak I am and is compassionate toward me, not angry at me.

Perhaps many of us take the second path, the path of walking away from God, because we feel guilty about our feelings toward God. We're not sure we can come to God with all of our painful, angry disappointment, so we don't come at all. Again, for most of us it's not a deliberate decision to walk away; it's more of an unchecked drift.

Questions about God, in light of our suffering, assault us day and night.

If God is good, why did he let this happen to me (or my family)?

If God is so powerful, why didn't he stop this from happening?

If God really cares, why doesn't he fix this?

Slowly but surely, all of the unanswered "why" questions undermine our confidence in God. It's not that we don't love him, we're just not sure we like him. We may not lose our belief in God, but secretly we're afraid we can't trust him anymore.

Frankly, some of our disillusionment is due to our one-dimensional thinking about God. We have correctly defined God as good, powerful, and caring, but we have wrongly interpreted that to mean he will always protect us from really bad stuff.

But that's not what he promised.

Your Story

Have you ever judged someone else without "walking a mile in their shoes"? Considering her losses, how do you feel about the outburst of Job's wife, "Curse God and die!"?

Have you found temptation to be stronger when you're enduring something painful?

Have you ever allowed yourself to be angry with God? If so, did it make you feel guilty or unspiritual?

Have you found yourself, intentionally or unintentionally, drifting away from God because of what you're going through?

13

Unclaimed Promises

We have a unique retail store in my neck of the woods that's become one of the most visited tourist attractions in the state of Alabama. It's tucked away in the northeastern part of the state in a little town called Scottsboro. The store is called *Unclaimed Baggage*. It's unique not because of what they sell, but how they acquire what they sell. In essence, they "claim" what other people don't, and then sell it. A whole lot of it!

Every week, they get several tractor-trailer loads of stuff that was left at baggage claims in airports and bus stations across the country. They sort through it, throw about a third away, give another third to charity, and then retail the rest. I recently had a chance to tour the facility with their CEO and get a behind-the-scenes look at the entire operation. It was impressive, to say the least.

But what impressed me most was the sheer volume of stuff that people never claim!

When it comes to pain and suffering, I think we leave a lot of Scripture unclaimed. I call these "unclaimed promises." By that I mean we naturally gravitate to the teachings in Scripture where God promises good things to his children. We embrace the promises of God about the abundant life, but overlook (or ignore) the clear teachings in Scripture that guarantee suffering as well.

Sometimes these promises are right next to each other, in the same passage of Scripture, but we sort of mentally edit them out. For instance, in Psalm 23, one of the best-known and most quoted psalms in the Bible, we learn:

God is my shepherd. *Claim. I'm all about that!*

I don't lack anything. *Claim. That sounds good.*

He gives me green pastures to rest in. *Claim. Resting in comfort is good.*

He leads me beside still waters. *Claim. No reason to risk drowning in whitewater.*

He restores my soul. *Unclaim! Sounds like my soul could be in bad shape.*

I'll walk through the valley of the shadow of death. *Unclaim! Sounds a little scary.*

He'll provide when I am surrounded by enemies. *Unclaim! I'd rather not have any enemies.*

You get the picture. It's not that we specifically, consciously "unclaim" those things, we just read over them glibly without really thinking about the implications.

Interestingly enough, though Job didn't have any Scripture to work from, he has a worldview that accepted both good and bad from the hand of God. Listen to his words in the wake of the unthinkable loss of all of his children, not to mention his financial catastrophe.

"The LORD gave and the LORD has taken away;
  may the name of the LORD be praised."
In all this, Job did not sin by charging God with wrongdoing.
(Job 1:21–22)

And then, after he's struck with a debilitating and disfiguring disease, his response to his wife's suggestion to curse God and die is, "You are talking like a foolish woman. Shall we accept good from God, and not trouble?" (Job 2:10).

I'm guessing the whole "You're talking like a foolish woman" thing probably didn't go over well. But his question, "Shall we accept good from God and not trouble?" is extraordinary in light of their situation. Job doesn't have a one-dimensional view of God that insisted God would only allow good in their lives. Furthermore, Job believes that everything they had was given to them by God, and as such, was his to take back at will.

We can learn a lot from Job on this one.

We can learn a lot from Jesus as well.

You see, Jesus didn't teach about a one-dimensional God either. He never promised that things would be rosy for his followers in this world. In fact, he promised them the opposite! Here's just a few of the promises Jesus said we could claim:

All men will hate you because of me.

You will be persecuted.

You will be tempted.

You will be arrested.

You will be flogged.

Some of you will be killed.

This is from the same guy who said, "I have come that you might have life and have it in abundance!" (see John 10:10).

Then, along with the aforementioned cheery personal promises, he makes some more general promises about bad things, saying they would come to every person in every generation on the face of the earth. He promises wars, famines, and earthquakes, and says these are only the beginnings of distress.

Here's the problem. A lot of us have read those things and assumed they would only happen to later generations. You know, people living in the end times. Not us.

Now it's interesting to me that Jesus doesn't go into an exhaustive explanation about why all this bad stuff is going down. Seems to me this would be the perfect time to give a little speech on why a good God allows suffering or why bad things happen to good people. You know, something?

Anything at all would be helpful.

But he doesn't.

He just says all these terrible things will happen. It's a promise.

And some of them will happen to good people precisely because they are good.

In John 15 and 16, Jesus warns his disciples about some of the really bad things that will happen to them (including execution) because they are his followers. Because they are doing right. Then he sums the whole thing up with this:

> I have told you these things, so that in me you may have peace. In this world you will have trouble. But take heart! I have overcome the world. (John 16:33)

Okay, would you walk me through that again, Jesus? You've told us all these really horrible things that will happen to us so we "may have peace"? How does that work?

Well, think about it. If Jesus had promised only good things would come our way, we should be in absolute shock when something bad comes. But since Jesus told us it was coming ahead of time, we shouldn't be shocked by it. It was promised.

But Jesus didn't say that peace was found simply in knowing that trouble was coming in advance. He said that "*in me* you may have peace" (italics mine). In him. In Jesus. In essence, he said, "In this world you will have trouble, but in me, you will have peace." He is pointing to a peace that comes in the midst of trouble, not the absence of it. A peace that passes understanding. A peace that doesn't make sense to others. A peace that comes from trusting him.

I always loved the verse my mom would quote to me from the Bible when I was anxious or afraid about something. "You will keep *him* in perfect peace, *whose* mind *is* stayed *on You*, because he trusts in You" (Isa. 26:3 NKJV).

A perfect peace comes in our perfect storms when we choose to focus on the promises of God—all of them—and trust him implicitly with the outcome.

We couldn't trust God if all he promised us was good stuff. He'd be untrustworthy. But we can trust God fully because he has promised both good and bad in this life. And we find a peace that passes understanding when we embrace both realities.

I mentioned earlier that we'd better not be too quick to crucify Job's wife. We'd better not be too quick to go and put Job on too big of a spiritual pedestal either. There's another forty chapters in the book. Chapters where Job:

> wishes that he were dead,
> curses the day he was born,
> insists God is out to get him,
> complains the wicked get off easy,
> and charges God with being unfair.

Not exactly the spiritual superhero we have sometimes imagined.

But think about his plight. He lost just about everything. His children, his career, his wealth, and his retirement plan. Now, on top of all that, he's lost his health. It's completely debilitating. Not only has he lost everything, he can't *do* anything. He can't eat, he can't sleep, he can't move. His life is comprised of sitting on an ash heap and scraping away at painful, blackening scabs. But perhaps even worse is what it means for his future.

He can't start over.

Welcome to the new normal.

Your Story

Have you ever given much thought to the fact that God promises us bad things will happen?

Are you surprised that Jesus didn't give more answers about why bad things will happen?

Have you found yourself frustrated that God hasn't answered most of your "why" questions?

How can the fact that Jesus promised trouble bring you peace?

PART 3

The New Normal

My days have passed,

my plans are shattered,

and so are the desires of my heart.

— JOB 17:11 —

14

There's No Going Back

How I long for the months gone by,
for the days when God watched over me.

Job 29:2

It's your first waking thought as your brain slowly moves from
pain-relieving sleep to dark, semiconscious reality.

Something's wrong.

Then you remember what it is. And it hits you like an emotional blitzkrieg, fresh pain from a wound that refuses to heal.

Every single morning.

If you've ever been through a perfect storm, you know exactly
what I'm talking about. You wake up every day in soul darkness. Sad. With a sense of dread. Maybe you're angry. And you
wonder if it will ever end. *Will I ever wake up happy again?*

It's awful.

I remember, during the storm when we lost our daughter, how
I absolutely dreaded waking up in the morning, which was weird
and highly unusual for me. Typically I was a morning person

who loved to get up early and greet each new day with a hot cup of coffee, my Bible, and a sense of adventure.

Not anymore.

Every day, my first waking thought was, *I don't have a daughter anymore*, followed by a dull pain in the center of my chest. Seriously. It felt like a mini–heart attack every morning. It created an emotional combination of both anger and deep sadness. It was miserable.

One minute your life's going along fine, and the next minute it's so irreparably ruined you don't want to go on living.

From light to darkness in a moment.

Kind of like a *haboob*.

Until about a week ago, I'd never even heard of this phenomenon. A *haboob* is a sudden, severe dust storm that moves rapidly and can engulf an entire city in a matter of minutes. Think major thunderstorm, with high winds hurtling dust and dirt instead of rain.

As I write this, Phoenix, Arizona, just experienced one of the worst *haboobs* in its history. I watched online videos of this event with wonder (and horror) as a massive, turbulent brown cloud closed in on the city and enveloped it. The city just disappeared. It was even more amazing to watch the videos shot by residents from their respective neighborhoods. One minute it was a beautiful, cloudless, sunny day, and a minute later it was midnight. You could barely make out the streetlights that had been automatically triggered by the darkness.

From light to darkness in a moment.

The kind of soul darkness I'm describing is like living in a never-ending *haboob*.

William P. Young personifies this ongoing emotional state as "The Great Sadness," and it's probably one of the most accurate descriptions I've ever heard. In his groundbreaking fiction book on God and tragedy, *The Shack*, Young tells the story of a parent whose young daughter has been abducted by a serial killer and never found. And every waking thought of every day for this father is consumed by a sense of loss and dread. Hopelessness.

The Great Sadness.

My eyes filled with tears when I read those words. I know that place. It's a bad place to be. The worst part is, it can go on for a long, long time. I mean, it's one thing to have a bad day. It happens to all of us at some point. Maybe even a bad month. Or year.

Try having a bad decade.

That's probably not what you want to hear right now, but for some kinds of pain there are simply no quick fixes.

About ten years ago, I watched one of my closest friends go through the agony of his eighteen-year-old son being diagnosed with an inoperable brain tumor. The family's lives were miserable for the next two years. They endured weekly trips to the hospital for almost lethal chemotherapy and radiation that promised to jeopardize his future if he ever recovered. Weekly trips to the emergency room became daily trips because of deadly complications associated with his treatment.

It was unbelievable.

That friend was the one who introduced me to the whole concept of a "new normal." About a year into their perfect storm, I remember driving up to his house in Wears Valley, Tennessee, about a half-mile outside of the Great Smoky Mountains National Park. I had suggested we take a hike up to the top of Mount LeConte, one of the tallest peaks in the park. I didn't know exactly how to be a friend to him during this season, but we had always loved hiking and backpacking, and I figured a break would probably be good for him.

It was an eye-opener for me.

As we hiked up the long trail to the top, I did about the only thing I could do: I listened. A lot. His daily life was best described as living in crisis mode, handling one crisis only to turn around and deal with another. There was incredible financial strain. How were they ever going to pay for this? The bills for the cancer treatment could be in the hundreds of thousands. And it was unclear how much their insurance would pay. It seemed that they would be saddled with medical bills unpayable in their lifetime.

But far worse were the health problems associated with his son's treatment. Because of the aggressive nature of the tumor, the chemotherapy had to be aggressive and was life-threatening in and of itself. His son immediately lost all of his hair and began rapidly losing weight. Because he couldn't keep any food down, they had to attach him to a feeding tube every night so that he wouldn't shrivel away to nothing. The radiation was equally aggressive.

Imagine intentionally exposing your brain to nuclear fallout on the scale of Chernobyl.

The radiation began to do irreparable damage to his nervous system, causing a loss of equilibrium. It also did severe nerve damage in his feet. The combination made it very difficult for him to walk—not that he felt like it anyway. That side effect alone created a whole new emotional pain for my friend. One of his greatest loves was hiking and trail running with his son.

That was out.

Then there was the hemorrhaging. Because of the radiation and chemo, his son was subject to sudden episodes of uncontrollable bleeding. One night, about two in the morning, they were awakened by cries from their son. They ran into the living room to find him covered in blood. He'd had a nosebleed and couldn't get it to stop. He couldn't get up, so his father hoisted him in his arms and carried him to the car. The hospital was over an hour away and they couldn't wait for an ambulance. They rushed him to the hospital, running red lights and praying that God would spare their son.

That was just one of many horror stories my friend shared that day.

As we headed down the mountain late in the day, I remember asking my friend when he thought his life would ever return to normal. I'll never forget what he said. "Our life will never be normal again. We live in a new normal."

I began to understand why my good friend was so sad all the time.

Honestly, my first thought was that he'd surrendered to an understandable cynicism about the future, and even about God. But in retrospect, I realized there was a tremendous amount of wisdom in his words. He knew he couldn't fix this. He'd come to grips with the reality that he'd never be able to go back to the fairly sane and stable life he knew before.

There is no going back.

When hardship comes, there's an intense desire on our part to get things back to normal as soon as possible, even if normal wasn't that good. When the children of Israel were finally freed from captivity to Egypt, they began to endure some painful trials associated with living in the desert. Food was scarce, and water even scarcer. As a result, Egypt started looking really good and they wanted to go back.

To slavery.

That always seemed such an odd thing to me. Even though it meant the loss of their freedom, being dependent on slave masters in Egypt seemed more reliable than being dependent on God in the unknown. At least they would know where their next meal was coming from.

Sara Groves wrote about this reality in her song *Painting Pictures of Egypt*. She describes her own painful journey, a journey so painful she found herself trying to "repaint" pictures of Egypt to make it seem better than it was, of wanting to go back to her old life even if it wasn't that good.

When we can't see our way ahead, or when what we do see in front of us looks really hard, we all tend to look back. We want to get back to the things we know, because they're comfortable.

There's no going back.

But they stunt our growth.

Many of us are familiar with Romans 8:28. You know, how God is going to work out everything for our good. (Again, this is one of those promises we claim.) But most of us don't remember verse 29, where it says God is determined to conform us to the image of Christ, to make us like his Son Jesus. And just as Jesus learned through suffering, so must we.

There was no going back to Egypt. God had something far greater for his children than comfortable bondage. The same is true for us.

There's no going back.

Job and his wife have lost everything and there is no getting it back. They are forced to a place in life they've never been before, and they don't like it. Job's life now consists of endless days sitting on an ash pile eaten up by boils, followed by sleepless nights interrupted only by panic attacks and nightmares.

Job is in a bad place. Every waking thought is consumed with the desire to go back. Back to when things were good, when he had financial security, when he enjoyed the company of his children, when he and his wife smiled at the thought of grandchildren . . . lots of them.

Back to "the days when God watched over me" (Job 29:2). But those days are gone, from Job's perspective. The problem for Job isn't simply that he couldn't go back. It's compounded by the fact he couldn't go forward either! It's kind of hard to rebuild your life when your health is so bad you can't move.

I mentioned earlier that I think Job's wife gets a bad rap for being an emotional basket case and giving up on God. But in a similar way, I think Job has been glamorized by Christian culture as being this incredibly patient man in the wake of adversity, almost robotically unemotional about his suffering. Others would paint a picture of him on top of his ash pile with a broad smile on his face, "just waiting for God to come through!"

But that's not the picture Job paints. Chapter 3 begins with these words: "After this, Job opened his mouth and cursed the day of his birth" (v. 1). When Job comes face-to-face with the harsh reality of his future prospects, he wishes he'd never been born.

But here's one of the most shocking statements Job makes during his new normal: "I prefer strangling and death, rather than this body of mine. I despise my life" (Job 7:15–16).

Strangling and death? We've all heard about the patience of Job, but if I didn't know better, I'd think Job was downright suicidal.

Turns out Job's human after all.

Your Story

Have you experienced "The Great Sadness"? How long did it last? Are you still there? Write about it.

Have you found yourself living in the past, fantasizing about the days gone by, perhaps desperately wanting to go back to them?

What do you think about the term "comfortable bondage"? Have you been there before? Is it possible you're there now?

God is always beckoning us forward, not backward. Where is he calling you to take a step forward with him?

15

I Want to Go Home

> Why is light given to those in misery,
>   and life to the bitter of soul,
> to those who long for death that does not
>   come?
>
>   Job 3:20–21

I wondered if I was losing my mind.

Am I becoming suicidal? I find myself fantasizing about heaven all the time. Not fantasizing about death exactly, but certainly about not being here anymore. I'd just as soon Jesus came back today. I'm tired.

I want to go home.

This was how I felt after we found out the little girl we'd loved so much would never be coming home to us again. The Great Sadness was smothering me. I was depressed and angry, and felt hopeless most of the time. I just wanted to go home. I can relate to Job, who longed for death that did not come. Maybe you've been there. Maybe you're there right now.

It's not such a bad thing. In fact, it can be a good thing.

Before you write me off as the next "Dr. Death," let me explain. There's a huge difference between longing for heaven and contemplating suicide. There are some similarities, to be sure. Both demand your life here come to an end. Both are an escape from pain. And both are selfish, to a certain extent. But there are some huge differences between the two.

One is healthy. One is unhealthy.

Here's what I mean. Suicidal thoughts are a bad thing, often driven by a subconscious, self-loathing, "the world would be better off without me" kind of mind-set. It's not simply a dissatisfaction with this world but an acute dissatisfaction with self.

Unhealthy, hopeless, not good.

I'm not arguing that those thoughts aren't understandable considering one's circumstances, but they're still bad and are fundamentally based on a deception. They lie when they declare there is absolutely no hope in my circumstance, that things will never get any better, and that somehow things will be better if I just take my life. In reality, such thoughts are incredibly selfish because suicide would just create an all-new storm others would have to deal with.

However, when suffering brings us to the point of a healthy dissatisfaction with this life, it can be a good thing. This life is not what we were made for. We were made for eternity. As such, we long for our true home, our heavenly home. Paul put it this way: "Meanwhile we groan, longing to be clothed with our heavenly dwelling" (2 Cor. 5:2). He also said, "If only for this life we have hope in Christ, we are to be pitied more than all men" (1 Cor. 15:19). In other words, if all we're living for is here and now, we're pitiful.

The psalmist Asaph went through a season of suffering in his life, "When [his] heart was grieved and [his] spirit embittered"

(Ps. 73:21). During that season he wrote, "Whom have I in heaven but you? And earth has nothing I desire besides you. My flesh and my heart may fail, but God is the strength of my heart and my portion forever" (vv. 25–26).

Asaph's suffering led to dissatisfaction with the things of earth but intensified his desire for God. The things of this world had lost their luster and created a longing for God, his "portion forever." The writer of Hebrews speaks of people who lived by faith, yet never received all that was promised in this life. "Instead, they were longing for a better country—a heavenly one. Therefore God is not ashamed to be called their God, for he has prepared a city for them" (Heb. 11:16). One day, beyond here and now, our faith will become sight and we'll experience the restoration of all things.

I want to clarify one more thing: there is a difference between what we feel and what we truly believe. Feelings are valid, but they may not accurately reflect reality. I believe suicide is driven by the feeling of hopelessness. Job experiences feelings of hopelessness and expresses them. In chapter 17, he laments, "Where then is my hope? Who can see any hope for me?" (v. 15). But I don't think Job is suicidal. He found little to hope for in this world, but he has hope in God.

One of the things I found to be healthy during my new normal was to express my feelings, even if they didn't seem particularly spiritual. Job's emotions are given in full voice to God and to others. Here's just a few of the choice one-liners Job throws out during his new normal:

"If I say, 'I will forget my complaint, I will change my expression, and smile,' I still dread all my sufferings" (9:27–28).
"I loathe my very life; therefore I will give free rein to my complaint and speak out in the bitterness of my soul" (10:1).

"All was well with me, but he shattered me; he seized me by the neck and crushed me. He has made me his target" (16:12).

That's simply how he felt. Maybe you have felt that way too. I know I have.

Honest Prayers

During that season of loss, I wasn't sure what to do with all of my feelings. I didn't feel much like praying, but one of our family disciplines was to pray every night with our five-year-old son. I didn't want to just stop praying with him altogether, but I was tired of trying to act or sound more "spiritual" than I really was.

So my prayers were typically very short. In fact, the night we gave up our daughter, it was just three words.

God, help us.

My son was a little bewildered. Even a five-year-old knows when a prayer is a little too short. Shouldn't there at least be a "God is great and God is good" stanza in there somewhere?

But it was the only prayer I could pray with any integrity. Some nights I would end my prayers with, "Even so Lord, come quickly." *Just take me home. There's nothing worth living for down here anymore.* My wife probably thought I was going over the edge. And in truth, I was. It was the first time in my life that I had ever truly *felt* despair and hopelessness.

But I was determined to be honest with God and others. My prayers with other family members or members of our congregation were the same: short, with a consistent plea for Jesus to return soon. In fact, now would be fine. I'm not sure what others thought at the time, but I have learned that praying like this is a good thing.

Before that experience, I couldn't relate to many of the psalms. David seemed like such a whiner! He was always upset with God about something, complaining about his lot in life. I thought it was a little blasphemous to talk to God like that. Not anymore. God is not offended by our honest prayers.

Now I know there are some who will call me a heretic for saying this, but here goes anyway: *maybe we have higher expectations of ourselves than God does.*

Maybe we have higher expectations of ourselves than God does.

I can't tell you how many times I've counseled those in extreme pain who, in a moment of emotional honesty, vent all of their angry disappointment with God . . . and then kind of duck, like they were expecting a lightning bolt from heaven! They feel badly about what they said, and quickly apologize to me as though no good Christian should—or even could—have those thoughts.

But there's no apology necessary. I'm quick to assure these wounded people that I'm a human being just like them and have felt most of the same things. Here's the beautiful thing about Jesus coming to earth and dwelling among us: he not only understands the human condition on a detached intellectual level, he actually relates to it from personal experience.

Again, remember what Hebrews says, that "we do not have a high priest [Jesus] who is unable to sympathize with our weaknesses. . . . Let us then approach the throne of grace with confidence, so that we may receive mercy and find grace to help us in our time of need" (4:15–16).

I love that! In my moments of greatest pain, I can come boldly to the throne of God and vent all of my anger and confusion and disappointment and know that he hears me. He is not offended by my frail humanity—he can actually relate to it! Perhaps many of us miss out on being comforted by God, receiving his grace and mercy, because we're afraid to come into the presence of God with complete honesty.

I absolutely love Psalms now. I turn to them often. They teach me to pray. They bring new meaning to the instruction, "cast all of your cares on him." God can handle it.

And that promise yields hope.

When things are bad, God reminds us through the apostle Paul that "hope that is seen is no hope at all. Who hopes for what he already has? But if we hope for what we do not yet have, we wait for it patiently" (Rom. 8:24–25). This is a profound teaching that helps us get through the new normal. We're hoping for something—something better.

The very essence of hoping is not having. Not yet anyway. To receive what we hope for demands waiting. Part of the perfecting work God is intent on accomplishing in our lives will only come through endurance. And it's in the waiting that we learn to hope.

This is not simply hoping for better circumstances but hoping in God, no longer only trusting in God based on what he does or doesn't do for us. Just trusting God. Trusting that whatever we are going through will finally work together for our good.

During his season of suffering and loss, Job learned to hope for something beyond simple prosperity in the here and now. He longed for death because he believed there was something beyond the grave worth hoping for. And no matter how bad his life was in the present, he knew his future, his eternal future, was promising.

> I know that my Redeemer lives,
>   and that in the end he will stand upon the earth.
> And after my skin has been destroyed,

> yet in my flesh I will see God;
> I myself will see him
>   with my own eyes—I, and not another.
>   How my heart yearns within me! (Job 19:25–27)

I don't believe Job thought his life was ever going to get better, at least not in the here and now. I think he had resigned himself to a life of bitter suffering. But he steadfastly believed a better day was coming! In the end, after he died, there would be a resurrection. A resurrection into new physical life and eternal prosperity.

This longing for the next realm, our resurrected life with God, is such a good thing! So much good can be birthed from dissatisfaction with this life. But frankly, to be dissatisfied with this world seems abnormal to most people.

Perhaps it's time we redefined normal.

Your Story

Have you ever found yourself longing for your heavenly home? Did it seem somehow wrong or unspiritual?

Have you allowed yourself to be honest with God in prayer— I mean completely honest?

What are some of the things you're hoping and praying for right now?

Do your prayers reflect that the majority of your hope in God is based on what happens in this life?

16

Redefining Normal

It was during this season of suffering that God forever changed what my "normal" was. Even though I didn't feel like it most mornings, I would still open my Bible and do a little perfunctory reading. I had no real anticipation or sense of purpose—more a sense of desperation. Even though I was disappointed with God, at some level I also knew I needed him now more than ever. One of these mornings, I was reading along in 1 Peter when I stumbled on 4:12, where Peter said, "Dear friends, do not be surprised at the painful trial you are suffering, as though something strange were happening to you."

Whoa, hold that coffee just a minute.

Do not be surprised at the painful trial you're suffering.

In other words, this shouldn't be such a shocker, Bruce.

Quite the opposite, in fact.

As though something strange were happening to you.

What's the opposite of strange? You guessed it. Normal. God points out that suffering is *normal* for believers. Not exactly what I expected when I signed on to this whole "following Christ" thing.

Talk about fine print.

There is a temptation to think of the Christian life as largely free from tragedy and serious pain. But that's a truncated gospel that leads to disillusionment and, for some, a complete loss of faith. Abundant life with God includes both joy and sorrow, victory and defeat, gains and losses. It's actually abnormal to experience a life free from pain and suffering.

Did you catch that? It's *abnormal*. And that's certainly not what God desires for us.

Notice I said it's not what God *desires* for us. I don't know about you, but there's a part of me that would gladly settle for abnormal, if abnormal means freedom from pain and heartbreak. I desire that freedom. Most days my heart would gladly set that as its noblest goal.

But there is a nobler desire that transcends our desire for circumstantial happiness. And this desire is only birthed through suffering.

It's the desire for God.

Not the desire for God to take care of me. Not the desire for God to fix it. Not the desire for what God *does* at all.

The desire for him.

True Desire

Here's part of the reason I say it's the grace of God that allows suffering. Without suffering, I would happily settle for having all of my lesser desires fulfilled. You know, a good family, a good job, good health, and some good friends. Circumstantial happiness.

And in all of that, I would probably trust God. I would still read my Bible, pray regularly, and participate in God's work.

But would I desire God?

Here's a sobering reality that I've had to come to grips with in my own life: my desire for God, when things are going well, can become more of a desire for God to keep things going well. In other words, I participate in the relationship in an unconscious effort to keep my life normal. At least, normal as defined by the world, and perhaps by most Christians.

Even some Christian leaders.

This is one of many reasons I have such a problem with the so-called prosperity gospel. It argues that circumstantial prosperity is the mark of God's blessing. God wants you to be happy, healthy, and wealthy. This is what's normal.

So if you are experiencing something "abnormal" like unhappiness, suffering, or bankruptcy, you are faced with one of two possibilities: you are either doing something wrong or, heaven forbid, God is.

Satan must love the prosperity gospel.

Think about it. What better way to keep people distant from God? If we are experiencing circumstantial prosperity, then God is acting right and apparently so are we. Our health, wealth, and prosperity prove it. God is just keeping his part of the bargain. In actuality, our hearts may be far from God, and our prosperity and pride are idols that keep us distant from God. We're smug and self-righteous—and Satan wins.

On the other hand, if we're experiencing suffering, pain, loss, or financial hardship, that obviously can't be God's will for us. So we must be doing something wrong, not exercising enough "faith," not pleasing God somehow, and so forth. God is acting right, so we must be acting wrong. In this case, our suffering creates a false sense of shame that keeps our hearts distant from God. We're guilty and ashamed—and Satan wins again.

But neither of these scenarios are the primary reason Satan loves the prosperity gospel. Oh no. These are good, to be sure, even effective. Both do a decent job of stunting our spiritual growth. The only problem with them, from Satan's perspective, is that we'll keep trying to do what's right! If things are going well, we'll do right to keep them going well. If things are going badly, we'll try to do right, partly to ease our sense of guilt but mostly to get things going well again.

But the most diabolical reason Satan loves the prosperity gospel is that it has the potential to absolutely shipwreck someone's faith.

Here's why. Say I'm doing the best I can to follow Christ, to live a life pleasing to God, and things go south—I mean really south. If I believe that God's primary desire for me is to be healthy, wealthy, and happy, then I can only come to one conclusion: God's doing something wrong.

I'm living right, so I should be experiencing God's blessing: circumstantial prosperity.

He owes me. That's how it works.

If he even exists.

The thought creeps into our subconscious. We don't allow it to form in our conscious thought. Not yet, anyway. But it's there, in the background, struggling for attention.

But even if we never get to the point of doubting the existence of God, we begin to doubt if we can trust him. I think we'd be shocked to know how many people over the centuries have lost their faith in God because something terrible happened to them and God didn't intervene. Their son died. Their spouse left them for someone else. Their daughter was raped. Their business went bankrupt. An accident left them paralyzed. Their father abandoned them. Someone lied and they went to prison.

So even if God exists, he certainly can't be trusted.

Shipwrecked faith.

All of this stems from a misunderstanding of what is normal. We would do well to remember that Jesus prayed for many things during his life on earth. And Scripture records that while his prayers were always heard, they were not always answered, at least not with a yes.

> During the days of Jesus' life on earth, he offered up prayers and petitions with loud cries and tears to the one who could save him from death, and he was heard because of his reverent submission. Although he was a son, he learned obedience from what he suffered and, once made perfect, he became the source of eternal salvation for all who obey him. (Heb. 5:7–9)

On the night Jesus was to be betrayed and then crucified, he pleads with the Father "to let this cup pass" from him. And God gives him the answer. No. But in answering no to Jesus's prayer, God said a resounding yes! to all of us who would benefit from his sacrifice. Eternal salvation.

In that sense, there is always a yes in God's no. I can't always see it, or understand it, but a benefit is coming, for me and for others.

One of the personal benefits that comes from suffering might seem strange to you, but it's one of the greatest gifts God has given me over the years.

Desperation.

Your Story

How do you feel about the statement that it is abnormal for Christians not to experience pain and suffering? Would you describe your life to this point as normal or abnormal?

Have you found yourself consciously or unconsciously buying into some form of the prosperity gospel? Does it surprise you to know that God the Father said no to at least one of Jesus's prayers? What can you learn from Jesus's experience?

How would you rate your personal desire for God right now—not the desire for God to do something, just the desire for God himself?

17

Desperate for God?

I cry out to you, O God, but you do not answer.

Job 30:20

Ever heard the worship song, "I'm Desperate for You"? Great song. I really like it.

It's not true for me. Most of the time, anyway.

During my new normal, I began to realize that even my approach to avoiding temptation and sin was driven more by a desire to keep bad things out of my life than a desire to please God. And part of that is good. Sin has its consequences and I've been far enough down that road to know that I don't want to go there. But avoiding sin and its consequences is different than desiring God. In some ways, it's really just a subtle form of control. Circumstantial control. Over God.

I am learning there's an "upside" to our fallenness. Falling to temptation and sin have made me far more desperate for God. And at the risk of sounding terribly unspiritual, I have to say that's a good thing. Here's what I mean: Jesus said, "Blessed are those who hunger and thirst for righteousness" (Matt. 5:6). The times when I have been the most hungry and thirsty for righteousness have been right on the heels of sinning!

Now before you write me off, let me explain. There have been several times in my life when I have royally blown it. I don't mean I made a little exaggeration and was confronted on it. I mean I flat-out lied and then tried to cover it up. I'm talking about those times when I deliberately sinned and then faced consequences that were potentially devastating for me and for others.

I can distinctly remember my feelings of guilt and shame—and a desperate desire for God to protect me from my own sin. I can remember praying like I've never prayed before, pleading with God, for my sake and for the sake of others. And it was genuine, a heartfelt desire for God to do something.

But it wasn't the desire for God.

Perhaps David recognized this tendency in his own heart. Psalm 51 is his prayer after being confronted by the prophet Nathan about his sin with Bathsheba and the subsequent murder of her husband. Bad stuff. Really bad stuff. And David pleads with God for mercy and for forgiveness, and not to be treated as his sins deserve. You and I would too! But in the middle of that prayer, I think we can sense the heart of David, pleading for that which he recognizes as most important, the thing that defines him as a man after God's own heart: "Do not cast me away from Your presence" (Ps. 51:11 NKJV).

In that moment of suffering the awful consequences of his sin, including the loss of his son, David recognizes what matters most to him: the presence of God in his life. Not the absence of suffering, and not freedom from the consequences of sin.

Remember that David is the king of Israel, arguably the greatest king before Jesus. But he doesn't plead with God not to take his kingdom away.

Do not cast me away from your presence.

He pleads with God not to take himself away.

This is perhaps the most remarkable difference between David and Saul. When the prophet Samuel confronted Saul with his sin of disobeying God, Saul pleaded for his kingdom.

Saul said, "I have sinned. But please honor me before the elders of my people and before Israel; come back with me, so that I may worship the LORD your God" (1 Sam. 15:30).

In other words, "Help me save face with the people. Help me protect my kingdom. Let's get things back to normal. Then I can worship God!"

Saul wants to get everything back to normal, the sooner the better. His worship depends on it. Perhaps his most indicting words are, "so that I may worship the LORD *your* God." We get the sense that Saul knows he is estranged from God, and that God has removed his presence from him. He actually describes the Lord as being Samuel's God, but not his own. And in this moment, when his kingdom is being stripped from him, he pleads with Samuel to save his kingdom so he could worship God again.

I'm a lot like Saul.

I can vividly remember when my kingdom was being stripped away from me. It was one of several storms that combined during my perfect storm. And I can remember my prayers all too well.

I told you earlier about a time in my life when I was leading a church and made some terrible decisions. These decisions had some unforeseen consequences. One of those consequences was that I was removed from my ministry position for a minimum of six months to undergo counseling and to do some real soul-searching. During that season of my life, God stripped everything away from me that I had held so closely: my reputation, my financial security, and my church.

I wasn't even aware of the idolatry in my heart until I lost my idols.

Up to that time, I was a respected young leader in our community, a real mover and shaker—a man of God who was going to be used greatly in our city. Seven years before, my wife and I had left everything behind and moved to Huntsville on the strength of our faith to plant a new church. We had no sponsoring church, no job, no savings, no house, and no congregation. Just the call of God on our lives . . . and a dream.

And that dream became a reality. The church flourished. The press reports were good. Bruce Martin was an up-and-coming spiritual leader in the city. I was asked to lead prayers at civic events and speak at meetings. I was honored by others in the community. I was asked to serve on the steering team for the local pastors' association. My reputation as a spiritual leader was growing, and so was my influence.

And I was digging it.

When the news of my sin became public, however, the press reports changed. *What a shame. He had so much potential. How could he have done such a thing?* I went from up-and-coming to down-and-out in about four weeks. My reputation was shot. I was now the loser pastor in our city. When people from the church would see me at the mall, they would pretend they hadn't and then duck into stores to avoid interaction. I definitely wasn't asked to speak anywhere or pray for anything.

The thing I remember sensing the most from others was disappointment. That was painful in and of itself.

But there were practical consequences as well. During this season when I was out of ministry, my church went through some understandable upheaval. Many folks left the church. The congregation dwindled and so did its financial support. I knew the church was about to go through some hard times financially because of my sin, and I didn't want my failure to put other staff members in jeopardy. So I asked the church not to pay me any salary as I went through my restoration process. It wasn't that noble, really. I didn't feel the church should be paying me a salary, so even though they insisted, I refused. I actually tore up the first paycheck they tried to give me.

I was in a deep state of depression and didn't even look for other work. Getting out of bed every morning was sporty enough. So we went for about seven months with no salary at all. We were going to counseling once a week to the tune of about $180 a session. Don't get me wrong—it turned out to be some of the best money I ever spent in the long-term, but in the short-term it was killing us. We amassed about $22,000 of credit card debt during that season. At a certain point, we were paying the minimum payments on our credit cards with our credit cards, so that we could keep using the minimum amount of credit that payment made available on the card. Confused? I hope so. It means we were about thirty days from bankruptcy unless something changed!

You don't realize what an idol financial security is in our culture until you lose it.

But in both of these areas, the loss of reputation and the loss of financial security, I still held on to some hope. I reasoned I could still get them back. I could rebuild my reputation in the community. I could turn around my financial situation. I could restore my broken world. My kingdom. My church. *I just need to get back to work!*

This brought me face-to-face with what I perceived to be the most devastating possible consequence: What if I didn't get a chance to go back to work? About five months into my restoration process, I received a letter from the elders of the church informing me, and the other members of the church, that they may not be asking me to return as their pastor. They were praying about initiating a search for another pastor.

Wow, I didn't see that one coming.

I was totally blindsided. I had never even considered that possibility. In every conversation with the elders and with my restoration team up to this point, I had never sensed that there was any question as to whether I would come back. There was only a question of when it would be appropriate. They had all unanimously agreed I had not disqualified myself from ministry, so steps were taken from that point on to restore me to ministry. In my mind, it was never a question of if I would come back, only when.

I remember reeling in complete shock. *Who do these people think they are? They can't just toy with someone's life like this! They can't just take it all away! Don't they remember? This church is my baby! I planted it, for heaven's sake! I've devoted six years of blood, sweat, and tears to this thing. It's my church.*

It's my kingdom.

I remember being gripped by a new fear. How was my wife going to handle this? I considered hiding the letter and not even showing it to her. She too was battling depression, clinging to the hope that I would be back to work in a few more weeks. Like me, she had never even thought of the possibility that I wouldn't be asked to come back. I had assured her over and over again that this was just a season and that soon we would have our life back. Back to normal.

I remember praying like I've never prayed in my life. "Please, God. Please. Give me another chance. I can fix all this. There's still a chance to redeem myself. Please don't take away my church."

Then I can worship you.

Looking back, this proved to be a major turning point in my life.

Like Saul, I was desperate to save my kingdom. Unlike David, I was not desperate for the presence of God.

But that time was coming.

Your Story

Do the words "desperate for God" sound appealing to you? Why or why not?

Have you ever associated the blessing of "hungering and thirsting for righteousness" with sin?

When you acknowledge sin in your life, does your prayer sound more like David's or like Saul's?

Pain and suffering have a way of revealing the hidden idols of our hearts. Are there any idols God might be revealing to you through your pain?

18

Control or Chaos

Let him do to me whatever seems good to him.

King David (2 Samuel 15:26)

When I was a kid, I used to love to watch the TV series *Get Smart*. It was all about control versus chaos. Literally. The good guys worked for a government entity called CONTROL, and the bad guys worked for a criminal network called chaos (spelled KAOS). And guess who always came out on top? That's right. Control wins again.

Because control is good, right?

Or is it?

There's a temptation to think it's all black or white when we're suffering, that control is good and chaos is bad. Therefore, we need to exercise control.

And exercising a certain amount of control in our lives is healthy. We get out of bed in the morning. We go to work. We don't say everything we think. We parent our children. You get the picture. That kind of control is good.

But there's also a bad kind of control. When you hear a daughter describe her mother as "controlling," you don't immediately think, *Now there's a personality trait I want to develop!* No, when you hear the word "controlling," you think, *Not good.*

There's nothing like a storm to make a person "controlling."

Most of us don't realize how strong our control tendencies are until we go through a major storm in life. But many of us will become certifiable control freaks during the new normal. Even if we begrudgingly accept the tragedy, we'll go through a season, consciously or unconsciously, of trying to fix things and get things back under control.

And that's understandable.

But the more we try to fix things and make them all better, the more frustration and disappointment we experience. Some things can never be fixed, or won't be "fixed" for a long time. Typically, control only makes things worse because it drives up our stress level exponentially. The expectations we had for our life before the storm have been destroyed, so we come up with new expectations. For ourselves. For our spouse. For our children.

I can fix this. Things are going to get better. I'll make sure of it!

At the very beginning of my perfect storm, before I had even resigned from the church, I spent a lot of time and emotional energy trying to "fix" things. The church wasn't going to disintegrate on my watch. But the more I tried to get my life back under control, some new wrinkle would be introduced that would set me back even further. That's partly where I learned things could always get worse.

Control is not our friend.

King David provides a vivid example of relinquishing control during a time of chaos late in his life. Most of the stories you've probably heard about David are about his victories and successes, and there were a lot of those along the way. But he saw more than his share of hardship too. Perhaps not quite as much as Job, but pretty close. Let's do a quick recap of some of his hardships, because I think they are part of the secret of where David's peace lies.

Pretty much as soon as God anoints David as the next king of Israel, his life gets really difficult. Sure, there's the whole "David and Goliath" story early on, but by and large for the next decade,

> *Control is not our friend.*

David is running for his life from the current king, Saul. After David finally does become king, he settles in Jerusalem, marries a bunch of wives, and has a lot of kids. But his family life looks a whole lot more like *Days of Our Lives* than *The Waltons*.

As I've already mentioned, one of his children dies as a direct result of his sin with Bathsheba. The painful regret he feels from that loss would be enough to drive most men insane. But then his son Amnon rapes David's daughter Tamar. Now, imagine what any father would feel in that situation. Sorrow. Anger. Weakness. It's a major catch-22. I mean, what do you do in a situation like that involving family members?

But things can always get worse.

Another son, Absalom, decides to take matters into his own hands (because Dad won't) and murders Amnon. So David spends the next several years completely estranged from Absalom, whom he loves deeply. On the counsel of others, he finally restores his relationship with Absalom. But as soon as he does, Absalom betrays him, sets himself up as king, rapes his father's wives, and sets out to kill Dad.

Talk about losing control.

His family is shattered, his kingdom is in jeopardy, and he's running for his life—again. His closest advisors are trying to convince him to take control again, including taking out his son.

David's response?

Let's pray about it. Maybe my time's up. Let's leave it in God's hands. In 2 Samuel 15:26 he said, "Let him do to me whatever seems good to him."

Let God do whatever seems best to him. I love that.

To some that sounds like a cynic who has resigned himself to a bitter fate. Maybe a disillusioned quitter.

To me it sounds like peace.

David understood the secret to peace in the middle of chaos: giving up control. No longer trying to dictate the outcome. Trusting God—no matter what, no matter when.

David had learned to trust the command, "Be still, and know that I am God" (Ps. 46:10). Typically our stress and worry are driven by the desire to control. Only as we give up control and choose to trust God no matter what the outcome can we experience a "peace that passes understanding."

So give it up. Chaos isn't always such a bad thing. Only on the other side of chaos can we understand the futility of control, anyway.

Losing it can be a good thing.

I remember a counseling session during my season of full-tilt "fix-it" mode, when I was still trying to minimize the trouble I had brought on the church and on my family. My counselor looked me in the eye and said, "Bruce, stop running from the pain. Embrace the pain."

Uh-oh. Time for a new counselor. This guy's lost his marbles.

Embrace the pain? I don't think so. Men don't embrace pain, we laugh at it. We mock it. We suck it up.

We intellectualize it.

He continued, "Bruce, you need to grieve."

In that moment, I began to realize that all of my running around, working so hard trying to fix things and make everything better, was really a desire for control. A desperate race to stay ahead of the pain that threatened to overtake my emotional stability.

"Embrace the pain. You've got to grieve."

Even as he said it, my eyes began to water. But immediately, some sort of "Don't cry" reflex kicked in. I couldn't do it. It wasn't that I didn't want to—I just couldn't.

It dawned on me then that I hadn't cried in years. Ten years.

Bitter emotions from the last ten years came rushing back like a torrent, threatening to overwhelm my sanity. For a long, long time I had been intellectualizing the painful parts of my journey and rationalizing them away instead of engaging with them at an emotional level. This comes naturally to most men. We compare our troubles to others and tell ourselves, *It's not that bad. Others have it worse, so what am I whining about? No sense dwelling on the past. Just suck it up and move on.* It's a survival mechanism, really.

We pastors are the worst. Not only do we intellectually rationalize away the pain, we spiritualize it too. You know, "God will work out everything for our good." And to a certain degree, we believe that.

Until we walk into something that doesn't work out.

Your Story

Can you relate to this intense desire to fix things when bad stuff happens? Does it seem strong or weak?

Have you ever associated stress and worry with control tendencies?

Have you allowed yourself to truly grieve your losses over the years or does it strike you as a waste of time and energy?

Where is God inviting you to relinquish control and simply trust him to do "whatever seems good to him"?

19

Losing It

My face is red with weeping,
deep shadows ring my eyes.

Job 16:16

Let me tell you a little about the birth of our twin boys and the beginning of our perfect storm. To do that I have to go way back, even before I was a pastor, because our storm began brewing the day we "decided" to have children. I laugh at that now, because we really thought we were in control of when and how our family would form.

Marlina and I had been married for about ten years when we thought it was about time to start a family. I had never really been crazy about having kids, and I thought our family was fine just the way it was. (This plays into my emotional state later, by the way.) But having children was hugely important to Marlina, so we began trying. There was an upside to this whole "Let's have a baby" thing. The joy of trying, if you know what I mean!

I know why they call it "trying" now.

It's not the same as succeeding.

And it can become very, very trying.

After about a year of trying and not succeeding, we took the advice of friends and got doctors involved. Now you've got to understand, I hate doctors. I don't mean doctors in general, but doctors' visits, doctors' offices, doctors' bills, doctors' probing and prying. In the world of infertility, it always makes sense to have the man in the equation checked out first. It's faster, easier, and less expensive.

And less invasive. Right.

The whole process seemed a little degrading to me, but I was determined to just get it over with. I had no concerns whatsoever about the actual test results. I come from a very fertile line of men in my family. I mean, my dad fathered six kids, for heaven's sake. And if my brothers even thought about sex, their wives turned up pregnant! So for me, this was a mere formality.

Until we got my test results back.

No swimmers. At all. Zero. Zilch. Nada. Dead or alive.

The doctors had no good explanation for this. They speculated that my, uh, reproductive system had gone into some sort of an early retirement. I was twenty-nine. Bottom line, there was nothing anyone could do. No treatments. Nothing.

I was sterile.

It's hard to explain all I felt that day. I think for women, it's probably impossible to understand. But I think men can imagine what I felt. It was a mixture of bothered, disappointed, sad, and keenly embarrassed. More embarrassed than anything though.

Sterile. *Impotent.*

Just writing the word makes me cringe. There's probably not a worse word you could ever use to describe a man, except for maybe coward, and frankly that wasn't looking so bad at the moment. The whole thing was demoralizing. I couldn't produce children. I couldn't give my wife the child she desperately wanted. And there would never, ever be a child on planet Earth that would share my DNA. But for me, the whole thing was just sad. And wrong. And unfair.

The worst part was I had to tell people about it, over and over again. Men and women. The whole thing made me sick. I really thought I would throw up if I had to tell one more person that we couldn't have kids because I didn't manufacture sperm! And as embarrassing as it was for me, you should've seen the looks on their faces. I could tell they had a lot more questions they really wanted to ask, but they just sort of said "Oh," and looked away.

Awkward.

Our only hope for having kids was some kind of adoption. Which sounds simple enough, until you actually begin trying to adopt. It's difficult, complicated, invasive, and expensive. Far more so than having a baby naturally. Oh, and insurance doesn't cover it.

So we started the process of a home study. For those of you not familiar with the term "home study," think major FBI investigation. There is no such thing as personal privacy in these matters. They ask every conceivable question about you, your family, your health, your past, your issues. . . . It's crazyville! Then they ask you questions such as, "Why do you want to have kids?" Well, let's see. How about, "Because my wife wants kids." Or how about this one: "Because normal people have children." Or my personal favorite answer, "It's really none of your business!" Of course, you can't actually give any of those answers if you want to "pass" the home study. They're looking for something more like, "Well, I've always wanted to have children so that I can express unconditional love and provide for the well-being of another human being."

The more personal questions I had to answer, the angrier I got.

At God.

I mean, come on, God. There are teenagers conceiving children in the backseat of a car somewhere and they don't even want children! Why does this have to be so hard for us?

Then there's the FBI check and fingerprinting. Seriously, we had to go down to our local police department, stand in line, fill out a form, and then get fingerprinted.

I felt like Al Capone.

In the middle of all this, we begin interacting with a prospective birthmother. I'll call her Dawn. Through a family connection, she learned that we want to adopt, so she made the decision to give us her baby. She was eighteen years old and had realized she was not ready to raise a child. She'd been in foster care almost all of her life because her father was in prison and she'd been separated from her mom for years. In fact, no one was really sure where her mom was.

So we hired an adoption lawyer to help us get it done. While any adoption is a complicated legal process, an interstate adoption is more difficult. So our lawyer recommended that we move Dawn to Alabama and establish residency for her. An already expensive process was becoming more so.

We rented a house for her. Because she'd been in foster care for so many years and never really had a father, I became a kind of surrogate father to her for the next six months. I helped her apply for a social security card, in-state medical benefits, food assistance, driver's license, and so forth. During this season, I really learned how important it is for a child to have a father. Dawn had never experienced things that I took for granted in my family. More than anything else, we wanted her to know that she and her child were loved.

All of this happened at the same time we were starting the new church. I survived by reminding myself this was short-term.

We just had to get through it until the baby came. I was trying to support my wife emotionally through all this, but I was also the only emotional support Dawn had.

My internal world started unraveling. I didn't know what depression was at the time, so I didn't know that's what I was lapsing into. I just knew I was irritable and angry all the time. I would keep my emotions in check around Dawn, but I would lose it around Marlina. Then I'd feel guilty and apologize, but it only added to the emotional strain. Inside, I was dying.

We found out that Dawn had not seen a doctor since she became pregnant, so we scheduled an appointment. She wanted Marlina and I to be in the room while she got her ultrasound, so we crowded around her bedside as the nurse prepared her for the procedure.

The nurse looked up at the monitor and said, "Here's baby A." Then she moved over to the other side of Dawn's belly and said, "And here's baby B."

Three people in the room went into shock. We sat there in stunned silence for a moment, then my wife blurted out, "Does this mean we get to keep both of them?" I stared at Marlina, eyes wide with my "I don't think you want to go there right now" look. Then I looked at Dawn, who was quietly staring at the monitor, looking almost mesmerized by what she was seeing.

Marlina and I quietly shuffled out of the room so Dawn could meet with her doctor. After the appointment, we all climbed back into our van for a silent trip home. I could tell something significant had taken place for Dawn, but I didn't know what.

I do know what happened to me though. I was finally excited about being a dad! Seeing those two baby boys on-screen changed me. Marlina and I immediately began to brainstorm names that would be fitting for twin boys. She came up with

Travis and Taylor. (She's got a country music strand somewhere in her DNA.) I came up with something a little more biblical: Elijah and Elisha.

No pressure.

We settled on Travis Elijah and Taylor Elisha, and they'd go by their first names. Christmas was just weeks away, so we put the word out to friends and family: "Buy stuff for boys, and buy twice as much!" We were both a little giddy. We'd hit the mother lode. Two for one. All of this was working out for good. It'd been hard, but it would be worth it.

We took Dawn with us to celebrate Christmas with my family. We were unsure if she had any family to spend the holidays with, and we didn't want her to be alone during this season. My family talked about her and the twins, how appreciative they were for her, and how excited they were for us.

But Marlina could tell something was wrong. She couldn't put her finger on it, but she knew. I told her she was just worrying for no reason—my typical response. But on the two-hour drive back to her rental house, Dawn didn't say a word. I started to think Marlina was on to something. Sure enough, about two weeks later, Dawn called us and said we needed to have a talk.

We knew what was coming.

She'd decided to keep her babies. She felt like God had given her something special and she was supposed to keep her boys.

We were devastated. We hadn't considered this possibility. Marlina was beside herself with grief. I intellectualized it and immediately jumped in and told her we'd be fine, throwing in something spiritual like, "We've got to trust God. It's going to work out for good."

Blah, blah, blah, blah, blah.

We told Dawn we would provide for the house and expenses until the babies came, and then one month after that so she could have her thirty-day postdelivery checkup. But after that she'd have to make plans to provide for herself and the twins. I was secretly hoping she'd realize that there was no way she could provide for herself, much less for two additional children.

About this time, Dawn's mother showed up out of nowhere and moved in with her. Apparently Dawn had located her mom and had been in communication with her for a while; we didn't know about it.

Marlina and I hadn't signed up for taking care of two people, but we did it, trying to do the right thing. I tried to say all the right things to my wife and others, maintaining the spiritual faith façade, but inside I was seething.

Two months later, Dawn went to the hospital for delivery. She gave birth to two healthy baby boys. While Dawn was in recovery, the nurse offered to let family members hold the new boys. Dawn's mother immediately said yes, but the nurse wasn't comfortable with letting her hold both of them at once, so she asked Marlina if she'd like to hold the other baby.

Time stood still for a moment. I was thinking, *Don't do it. This is a bad idea.* But Marlina, profoundly under the influence of God's grace, reached out her arms and took the child.

Tears formed in my eyes, but I dutifully choked them back.

I didn't cry until I got home. I remember sitting under a tree in my front yard, just crying, pouring out my heart to God. Acknowledging that my life was out of control and there was nothing I could do to fix it. The pain in my heart seemed unbearable.

I was finally desperate for God.

Not to "fix it," though. This situation wasn't fixable. I wanted the presence of God, the will of God, in my life no matter what.

As my tears flowed that day, peace from God began to flow in my heart as well. I didn't realize it at the time, but I was growing spiritually. My soul was deepening.

By the way, don't expect your friends to understand. Until someone has "been there, done that," they don't really know what you're going through.

Job came to know that firsthand.

Your Story

Have you ever found yourself comparing your hardships to other people who seem to be living a charmed, largely pain-free life? Did it create questions about the fairness of life? The fairness of God?

There is a certain degree of embarrassment associated with some kinds of suffering. Have you experienced embarrassment or shame as a result of your trial?

Have you had to endure a significant amount of hardship because you were trying to do the right thing? How did that make you feel?

Have you ever experienced peace when your life was totally out of control? Have you ever really surrendered control?

20

Well-Meaning Friends

> A despairing man should have the devotion
> of his friends,
> even though he forsakes the fear of the
> Almighty.
>
> Job 6:14

Most of the book of Job is a bunch of talking—about theology. It's like one long debate between seminarian wannabes. Now, don't check out on me because I used the word *theology*. The word simply means what a person believes about God. Everybody believes something about God, including atheists, so in that sense everyone is a theologian.

Including you.

And what you believe or understand about God is your theology.

The whole *story* of Job, the narrative, is told in chapters 1–3 and chapter 42. The intervening thirty-four chapters are theological monologues by Job and his friends, followed by a four-chapter theological monologue from God. We'll wait to unpack what God said, and focus on Job and his buddies for now.

By the way, Job's friends start off great! They mourn with him and don't say a word. Good call. If you've ever been through a perfect storm, you know how valuable this is. A person in mourning isn't ready to hear the wealth of your vast spiritual knowledge. They need you to be present, first and foremost, and to listen.

But after about a week of that, Job's friends decide it's time to set Job straight. In chapter 4, a great spiritual debate ensues that goes all the way to chapter 37. The debate is about how God works, and each friend gives his take on Job's predicament based on his limited understanding of God. Let me give you the *Reader's Digest* condensed version of those chapters.

Job's friends: Because God is just, good things happen to good people and bad things happen to bad people.

Job: Not so much.

Seriously. That's pretty much it. Thirty-four chapters of back and forth about the same thing. Job's friends are committed to their understanding of God, which was the prevailing theology of their time. One friend sums it up this way:

Consider now: Who, being innocent, has ever perished?
   Where were the upright ever destroyed?
As I have observed, those who plow evil
   and those who sow trouble reap it. (Job 4:7–8)

In other words, "Job, you can't be innocent. Good people get good things. Bad people get bad things." Essentially, a theological version of karma. What goes around comes around.

And you know what? Previous to this point in his life, Job might have said something similar. But this perfect storm really messed with his theology. As we saw earlier, Job's theology was expansive enough to accept both good and bad from the hand of God, but he still wanted to know why the bad happened.

Job knows that he's innocent of wrongdoing, so he asks God, "Why is all this bad stuff happening to me?" Job's friends know that God is just, so they assert that Job must have done something wrong. In truth, both Job and his friends were partly right and partly wrong.

Some people have the mistaken idea that Job's friends were wrong about everything and Job was right about everything. But Job's friends were right about some things: God is good, God is just, God can do whatever he pleases. Job was right too, as he believed those same things.

However, Job's friends were wrong in their assertion that God was punishing Job for some secret sin. And Job was wrong in his assertion that God was out to get him. They were all victims of an insufficient theology. Not bad theology, necessarily, just insufficient.

Interestingly enough, neither Job nor his friends ever considered the possibility that God is good and just, *and* sometimes bad things happen to good people because they are good.

Typically, neither do we.

Like Job and his friends, we have an insufficient theology. When tragedy strikes, we immediately wonder what we've done wrong to bring this kind of pain into our lives. Or, like Job, we begin to think that a fickle God is out to get us. Rarely do we think, *I'm on the right track! I must be doing something right to experience this kind of suffering.*

I said earlier that Satan must love the prosperity gospel. It's a great deception that actually distances people from God. Job and his friends had unwittingly bought into an idea that the goodness of God precludes suffering.

Fast-forward to the first century AD. Jesus's early disciples struggled to understand suffering through this lens as well. This was one of the major misunderstandings of God that Jesus had to address early on with his followers. They had the same basic idea that God was opposed to suffering unless someone deserved it.

Here's how it played out: Jesus would do all these incredible miracles, indisputably proving himself to be the long-awaited Messiah. He of all people was doing things right. Then he would dismiss the crowds, take his disciples aside, and tell them he was going to suffer and die. At one point Peter got so disturbed by Jesus's "suffering and dying" theme that he took Jesus aside and said, "Not so, Lord! This will never happen to you!"

I don't know about you, but I get kind of tickled at the thought of ever "taking Jesus aside" on something (even though I've done it myself a few times).

In essence, he was saying, "Jesus, you're the man! You're doing things right. God would never let that happen to you."

It didn't go as well as Peter probably thought it would.

Jesus looks at him and says, "Get away from me, Satan! You're not seeing this from God's perspective but from man's" (see Matt. 16:21–23).

Don't you just hate it when Jesus calls you Satan?

Now, why would Jesus say something like that? Because that's exactly what Satan wants us to think—that bad things only happen to bad people! He thrives on condemnation. He wants us to believe we must have done something terrible when we experience suffering. Or better yet, that God is out to get us. Either way, it's a win-win for Satan. We live in false shame and guilt, or we believe God doesn't like us. Both make us feel far from God. Detached. Alone.

But over and over again, Jesus told his followers things like:

> Blessed are those who are persecuted because of righteousness, for theirs is the kingdom of heaven.
>
> Blessed are you when people insult you, persecute you and falsely say all kinds of evil against you because of me. Rejoice and be glad, because great is your reward in heaven. (Matt. 5:10–12)

This was such a consistent theme of Jesus's teaching it's actually pretty amazing that the disciples didn't get it! But we don't get it either. We tend to gravitate to teachings that we like, that suit our preformed theological ideas.

Only later in their journey, after they had experienced suffering and persecution, did the disciples get it. There's a great story in Acts 4 and 5 where you sense this teaching finally clicked for them. Peter and the apostles are proclaiming Jesus as Lord, the long-awaited Messiah. They're healing people from diseases and freeing people who had been captive to demonic forces for years. In short, they're doing good. But there were a bunch of people who didn't want a Messiah. They were quite happy with the lifeless religion they already had, and they didn't need a bunch of "do-gooders" to make them look bad. So they threatened them with their lives and said, "Stop it, or else!" They told the apostles that if they kept this up, they would do to them what they did to Jesus.

It wasn't an idle threat.

But Peter and the gang decided they had to obey God rather than men, so they kept at it—and as a result they were thrown in prison. Long story short, God miraculously released them from prison and they picked up right where they left off, preaching and teaching Christ and doing good. Then they were called back into the principal's office (the Sanhedrin) to be held accountable. Once again, they were threatened with their lives and told to shut up.

But this was their take on the whole experience: "The apostles left the Sanhedrin, rejoicing because they had been counted worthy of suffering disgrace for the Name" (Acts 5:41). They got it! Sometimes bad things happen because you're doing good. Not everyone, particularly Satan, appreciates those who do good. Later in life, as Peter reflects on his journey with God, he says, "even if you should suffer for what is right, you are blessed" (1 Pet. 3:14). Peter and the rest of the disciples were no longer victims of an insufficient theology. They were willing to claim all of the promises of God that included times of prosperity, healing, and joy as well as times of suffering, pain, and loss.

Job and his friends weren't there yet.

One of the most difficult things you will have to navigate when going through an extended time of suffering is how to deal with friends. When you're going through a long season of trouble, don't be surprised if your friends seem a little frustrated with your slow progress toward healing. The longer your pain lasts, the longer your storm is, and the longer you grieve, the harder it becomes for them to stay engaged. There's a subconscious (if not overt) desire on their part for you to get better. It's almost like they're pressuring you to get over it and get beyond it. When they ask how you're doing, they don't want to hear, "We're doing awful." They want to hear something like, "I'm really better," or, "We're doing okay."

Part of the reason they want you to get better is for you. Your friends genuinely love you and want you to be happy again, with your life returned to normal.

But part of it's for them. Seeing you suffer day after day, week after week, month after month is painful for them. I think this is why Scripture tells us to mourn with those who mourn. It doesn't tell us to fix it, or insist that someone get better, or put a certain time limit on mourning. It just says mourn with them.

As I've reflected on the whole discussion between Job and his friends, I realize this is part of what's fueling the intensity of the debate.

His friends want to get Job's life back to normal.

They may not want it as much as Job does, but they want it. You can hear it in their words. Over and over again they plead with Job, "Repent of your secret sin. Then God will forgive you and restore your life again."

If you'll just repent of whatever desperately wicked thing you've done, everything can get back to the way it was.

Including the friendship. They were ready for life to get back to normal.

But there was no secret sin. There was no "desperately wicked" thing for Job to repent of. There was no going back to normal, and Job knew it. Life would never be the same and he was tired of debating about it—at least with people.

After about forty chapters of arguing with his friends about the reasons for his suffering, Job asks for a little sit-down with God. Like us, he wants answers, but not from people with understanding as limited as his own. He wants the chance to take his case directly to God, to go head-to-head with the Big Man. He wants a shot at the title.

He wants his day in court. Divine court.

So he proclaims, "Oh, that I had someone to hear me! I sign now my defense—let the Almighty answer me" (Job 31:35).

Be careful what you pray for.

Your Story

Did it ever occur to you that the reason you are going through a difficult season is because you are on the right track?

Have you thought about the reality that your suffering could be producing reward for you in heaven?

What are some other potential blessings that come from suffering for doing right?

Does it seem to you that your friends don't understand your situation? Do you ever sense that they would like you to just get over it already?

PART 4

Searching
for Meaning

Then the Lord *answered Job out*

of the storm.

— Job 38:1 —

21

Brace Yourself!

Who is this that darkens my counsel
  with words without knowledge?
Brace yourself like a man;
  I will question you,
  and you shall answer me.

Job 38:2–3

Tired of unjust accusations from men, Job wants to take his case to the highest court: God's court. His charge? That God is unfairly out to get him. Job proclaims, "He would crush me with a storm and multiply my wounds for no reason" (Job 9:17). Now remember, Job doesn't have the benefit of reading the first chapter of the book that bears his name like you and I do. All he knows is what he sees. And what he sees is that he was a righteous man, following God's commands, doing the right things, and his life completely fell apart.

What gives?

In short, Job wants to know "WHY?" And finally, God answers. "Then the LORD answered Job out of the storm" (Job 38:1). I can imagine Job thinking, *Well, it's about time! Finally we're going to resolve this whole thing.* After all the suffering and loss and scab picking, Job would get some answers.

It's the day in court we all think we want.

It doesn't go so well for Job.

God begins with, "Who is this that darkens my counsel with words without knowledge? Brace yourself like a man; I will question you, and you shall answer me" (Job 38:2–3).

Hmm. "Brace yourself like a man." That can't be good. I don't know about you, but if God starts a conversation with me by saying, "Brace yourself!" I'm rethinking my need for answers. On top of that, God addresses Job as someone who "darkens his counsel" and speaks "words without knowledge."

Ouch. If I'm Job, I'm cringing a little already.

God then launches into a series of questions (because everyone knows you can't have a legitimate courtroom drama without a lot of questions). It's kind of like a divine version of "Twenty Questions," except it's more like "Eighty Questions." Eighty-two, to be exact. And these aren't your average "Are you smarter than a fifth grader?" questions. No, these are more like "Are you smarter than the God of the universe?" questions:

> "Where were you when I created everything?"
>
> "What are the exact dimensions of the cosmos?"
>
> "How about just the earth? Land and sea?"
>
> "Any word on the galaxies? How about stars? How many do you think?"
>
> "What about storms? Do thunder and lightning report to you?"

"What about animals? Do you know all about them?"

"Why does a mother goat leave its young alone in the wild?"

"Why does an eagle soar? Why is a stork so dumb?"

"Why does a horse charge into battle unafraid, but a cow not so much?"

You get the picture. In seventy-one verses, God peppers Job with fifty-eight questions to which Job has no answer. And God knows he doesn't. God is making a point about his wisdom. Mercifully, after two chapters of this, God gives Job a chance to speak. "The LORD said to Job: 'Will the one who contends with the Almighty correct him? Let him who accuses God answer him!'" (Job 40:1–2).

Okay, Job. You wanted to be a contender. It's your shot. What do you got?

(cricket chirp)

Nothing.

Job's got nothing. And he knows it. Rather than trying to bluster through like some of us might, here's his response: "I am unworthy—how can I reply to you? I put my hand over my mouth. I spoke once, but I have no answer—twice, but I will say no more" (vv. 3–5). Good answer. No answer.

Job does the smart thing. The honest thing. Job recognizes that the wisdom of God is beyond his comprehension. He can't possibly fathom the infinite knowledge of God. At this point, I think Job's hoping the conversation is over. I know I would.

But God continues, "Brace yourself like a man; I will question you, and you shall answer me" (v. 7).

I imagine Job's thinking, *No, no. We're good here.* But God's not quite finished. There's more that God wants Job to learn. God's made an airtight case for his wisdom and knowledge, but now he's going to address two other underlying issues Job is struggling with.

The issue of his justice and the issue of his power.

God said, "Would you discredit my justice? Would you condemn me to justify yourself? Do you have an arm like God's, and can your voice thunder like his?" (vv. 8–9).

You see, Job questioned God for being unfair to him. But there's a deeper question behind the question: If God was committed to being fair (at least as Job understood fair), then why didn't he do anything to alleviate or even prevent Job's suffering?

Was God powerless?

Again, God engages a long series of questions about his justice and his power. This time it's twenty-four questions about his power over man and beast. Any man and any beast.

He addresses the issue of his justice (and his power to effect that justice) by indicating his ability to "look at every proud man and humble him, crush the wicked where they stand. Bury them all in the dust together; shroud their faces in the grave" (vv. 12–13). In other words, there's no man strong enough to escape the justice of God by his own power.

God then begins to question Job about man and his power over animals. But these aren't questions about simple domestic beasts, like cows or sheep. Oh no. He asks about man's power over the two largest, most fearsome beasts of their day: the behemoth and the leviathan. Epic, mythical stuff.

"Look at the behemoth, which I made along with you" (v. 15). God starts by reminding Job that he made both behemoth and man. I think God is making a clear comparison about relative power here. Man versus behemoth. Who wins in that matchup?

Behemoth, hands down.

But what about God? God made a point about the behemoth being the biggest and strongest creature that he's ever created, and then said, "He ranks first among the works of God, yet his Maker can approach him with his sword" (v. 19). In other words, *you can't handle him, but I can.*

Right here's where God interjects a little humor. The proceedings to this point have been a little heavy, so God lightens up the mood with, "Can anyone capture him by the eyes, or trap him and pierce his nose?" (v. 24). What, you're going to capture a behemoth? Maybe keep him in a barn or something, or put him on display in a zoo?

I can see God smiling.

But the stand-up routine isn't over. Now God wants to talk about the leviathan for a minute, a full-tilt sea monster. He quips,

> Can you pull in the leviathan with a fishhook
>   or tie down his tongue with a rope?
> Can you put a cord through his nose
>   or pierce his jaw with a hook? . . .
> Can you make a pet of him like a bird
>   or put him on a leash for your girls? (41:1–2, 5)

I love it. God said, "Can you catch a leviathan like you would a fish? Are you going to make it a pet for your children? Rustle up a little pony for your daughter?"

You've got to admit. That's funny.

God makes his point clearly: *I am just. And at the end of the day, I will see that justice is served. For everyone.* And God makes the point that he's all-powerful; strong enough to do anything he pleases, with man or beast.

Got it.

But here's the part that's a little disappointing to me, and maybe to you too. At the end of the day, God doesn't give Job any answers to his questions.

None.

Not a single one. There's no, "Well, let me explain here . . ."
Nothing.

Just a lot of questions. Again, questions Job has no answer for.

In reality, God just gave him an even bigger list of unanswered questions. In essence, God said to Job, "I know you have unanswered questions. In fact, there are a lot more unanswered questions you haven't even asked yet. But know this: I am wise, I am just, and I am powerful. And I want you to trust me with your suffering and pain and loss."

Now at first glance, I thought this might create some frustration on Job's part. "God, I just wanted a simple answer: Why?" But listen to what he says in response.

> Then Job replied to the LORD:
> "I know that you can do all things;
>   no plan of yours can be thwarted.
> You asked, 'Who is this that obscures my counsel
>   without knowledge?'
>   Surely I spoke of things I did not understand,
>   things too wonderful for me to know." (42:1–3)

Job is not left frustrated by all of these unanswered questions. Instead, the sovereignty of God—his wisdom, his justice, his power—give Job a sense of peace, a peace that I frankly don't think he'd have if God had answered his questions. (How do you think Job would've felt if God tried to explain chapter 1 to him?) It is clear to Job that God is fully in control of the situation, and for him, that's enough.

In a similar way, God hasn't answered all my questions about my own suffering. Like Job, I don't have the benefit of reading chapter 1 of my story. I don't know what's going on behind the scenes. This is the essence of what it means to live by faith! To live by faith is to believe in the unseen, and to trust God in our troubles even when everything we see around us is bad.

This truth kept the apostle Paul going, even through some of his worst trials. He said,

> Therefore we do not lose heart. Though outwardly we are wasting away, yet inwardly we are being renewed day by day. For our light and momentary troubles are achieving for us an eternal glory that far outweighs them all. So we fix our eyes not on what is seen, but on what is unseen. For what is seen is temporary, but what is unseen is eternal. (2 Cor. 4:16–18)

I love that Paul is writing this. Of all people, Paul knew more than his fair share of suffering. In fact, when Jesus first called Paul to follow him, he said, "I will show him how much he must suffer for my name" (Acts 9:16).

Paul probably should have looked at the contract a little closer.

Throughout his life, Paul learned that God was far more intent on perfecting him through trouble than on protecting him from trouble. If anyone had reason to "lose heart," Paul did. He got into trouble everywhere he went. He spent most of his missionary journeys as a fugitive, fleeing from one city to the next. He was imprisoned numerous times, flogged severely, beaten with rods, and shipwrecked in a furious storm. Oh, and let's not forget stoned and left for dead!

To live by faith is to believe in the unseen, and to trust God in our troubles even when everything we see around us is bad.

And what was his take on all that? "Light and momentary troubles." Unbelievable. How could he say that? Because he knew they were achieving something glorious, something that would only be revealed in eternity! God was up to something behind the scenes that would make it all worth it someday. Paul survived his troubles, even thrived in them, by focusing on the eternal, knowing that every trouble he faced was only temporary.

I can't always see the bigger picture. But I do get glimpses of it from time to time. In the next several chapters, I'll share with you some of the "glimpses" God has given me in relation to suffering. They aren't answers, exactly, more like insights or even reflections, because there are certain things you can never really know until you have walked through them.

It's called hindsight.

Your Story

Have you ever wanted to have a little "sit down" with God and get some answers? How about now?

Have you ever wondered why God didn't exercise his power and stop something from happening to you?

Has your suffering brought you to the point of questioning the justice of God?

Does it bother you that God didn't answer any of Job's questions? Do you have some unanswered questions? Take time to write them down, here and now.

22

Hindsight Is 20/20

I will put you in a cleft in the rock and cover
you with my hand until I have passed by. Then I
will remove my hand and you will see my back.

Exodus 33:21–23

During our season of loss, God connected us to some excellent
Christian counselors who helped us navigate the pain and make
conscious steps toward healing. On one occasion, my wife and I
asked if there would ever be an end to our grief. It seemed that
our life was consumed with sorrow, a daily reminder of what
we had lost and could never get back. We were pretty deep into
our new normal, and didn't like it. Frankly, as a man, I was a
little tired of being reduced to tears so often.

I'll never forget what our counselor said. "The end of all
grieving is to find meaning."

He instructed us to look back and begin journaling about the
times in our life when we had experienced pain, loss, or suffering.
Then he challenged us to look for the work of God in our lives

during those times. The majority of what you're reading right now is a direct result of those journal entries. As I looked back, I could see some incredible things God did in my life, particularly in regard to character and leadership development. These were lessons I never would've learned any other way.

I began to understand.

Webster's dictionary defines *hindsight* as the "understanding of an event after it has happened." It's the reality that certain events can only be really understood *after* we experience them. Before we experience something, we only have a limited understanding of it. We may have certain ideas and opinions, but we can't really, truly understand until we go through it.

> *The end of all grieving is to find meaning.*

This is true for many of us regarding pain and suffering. Our understanding of God in relation to suffering has been formed well in advance of actually experiencing suffering, typically in our childhoods. Many of us learned of a God who loves us and who, because of that love, is our protector and provider. We come to believe that God's primary work, his greatest concern, is to provide for our needs and protect us from trouble. Unintentionally, even the best of parents can set their children up for major disappointment later in life if they paint only this one-dimensional picture of God.

The problem comes when the problems come. We're going through a tough time, we need provision, or we need protection . . . and we don't get it. Our preconceived notions about God, our insufficient theologies, crumble around us. And for many of us, our faith is shaken. There are certain things you simply can't know before you experience them.

But the meaning of hindsight goes even deeper than that. It also embraces the reality that while we're in the middle of something, we often still can't understand it. In fact, being in the middle can actually be the worst possible time to seek understanding, the proverbial "can't see the forest for the trees" dilemma.

Prolific writer and theologian C. S. Lewis experienced this phenomenon firsthand. For years he was one of the most acclaimed writers on the subject of God and suffering, and his book *The Problem of Pain* was a bestseller. But his perspective on pain and suffering blurred dramatically when he was in the middle of it.

When his beloved wife died of cancer at age forty-five, despite all of his prayerful pleadings, he said of God, "But go to him when your need is desperate, when all other help is vain, and what do you find? A door slammed in your face, and a sound of bolting and double bolting on the inside. After that, silence."[2] Just as our eyes are blurred by tears when we're in the middle of a great sorrow, our spiritual vision is blurred as well. We can't see clearly, and sometimes not at all.

We've all heard the quote, "Hindsight is 20/20." It's the idea that while we can't understand or "see" certain things clearly before or during an event, we can often see them quite well afterward. 20/20. Perfect vision, as it were.

There's a familiar story told in Exodus 33 about hindsight. Well, more like hind-side, seeing something from the back side. Moses is leading the nation of Israel out of bondage in Egypt and into the Promised Land. There are a million or so people involved and the whole trip is taking a lot longer than anyone expected. Understandably Moses is looking to God for guidance.

But he knows it's hard to get God's perspective on something in the middle of it. So he devises a clever way to get "outside" of the problem. "Now Moses used to take a tent and pitch it outside the camp some distance away, calling it the 'tent of

2. C. S. Lewis, *A Grief Observed* (New York: Seabury Press, 1961), 45.

meeting.' Anyone inquiring of the LORD would go to the tent of meeting outside the camp" (Exod. 33:7).

When Moses needed to hear from God on something, he had to get "outside the camp," some distance away from the problem. This option was available to anyone who wanted to hear from God, but we get the sense that Moses was out there a lot.

One time, Moses is out there chatting with God about leadership. The bottom line for Moses is that he can't do this alone. In fact, he's not going to go one step farther unless God promises to be with them—to be physically present with them. So God affirms his deep love for Moses and promises that his "presence" will go with them. They will never be alone.

Then Moses, almost abruptly, asks to see something: "Now show me your glory" (Exod. 33:18).

Moses wants to see the glory of God. Right now. It's almost like he wants to see everything, the full weight of God, the whole picture, the cosmic plan. To which God said, in essence, "You can't handle my glory! It's way too much for you. To see all of me now would kill you." But God graciously provides a way for Moses to see part of him, not from the front side but from the back side.

> Then the LORD said, "There is a place near me where you may stand on a rock. When my glory passes by, I will put you in a cleft in the rock and cover you with my hand until I have passed by. Then I will remove my hand and you will see my back, but my face must not be seen." (Exod. 33:21–23)

God said, "I'll protect you from what you can't see while my glory passes by, but then I'll give you a glimpse of my glory from the back side." The hind side. Hindsight.

So God presented himself to Moses and passed by him. However, while he was passing by, he carefully covered Moses with his hand, effectively hiding himself from Moses. Only after the event can Moses get a glimpse of God.

There's parallel to suffering here. In our most painful and difficult times in life, we desperately want to see the glory of God, to hear from him, to know he is there. But it seems like God is passing by, maybe even hiding from us. However, perhaps in reality he is covering us, protecting us in ways that we can't see or understand at the time.

Reflecting on this, it's made me wonder how often God has protected me in certain storms but I didn't know it. When the storm was raging, how many times did God intervene on my behalf, lessening its severity? When did God protect me in ways I can't possibly know? Therein lies the rub—I don't know. In fact, I can't know.

Here's another question about what's hidden from us in times of trouble. When did God work through our suffering to benefit someone else?

I told you the story earlier about the parents whose son had brain cancer. Let me tell you a little of the back story of how his cancer came to light.

Both my friend and his son are avid outdoorsmen and for years had dreamed of one day hiking all of the Appalachian Trail together. The trail is over two thousand miles long, so they would need a four- or five-month window to complete it. His son had just graduated from high school, and his contracting business allowed him the flexibility to take a significant amount of time off. The conditions were perfect. His son could take a year off school and then start college in the fall after they finished their adventure. If they were ever going to do it, now was the time. After months of saving and planning, in the spring they headed out from Springer Mountain, Georgia, with Mount Katahdin some 2,181 miles to the north in Maine.

Several months and over a thousand miles into their trip, the dad became gravely ill. He'd contracted giardia, an intestinal parasite, from an unfiltered water source along the trail, and he had reached the point where he couldn't keep any food down. His body weight dropped drastically, and with it, his energy level. He was reduced to hiking slowly for a couple of miles or so, then collapsing into his tent. After several weeks of intense suffering, trying desperately to finish what they'd started, he realized his body couldn't go any farther. His trip was over.

But what about his son?

They made the painful decision at a shelter in Pennsylvania, about a mile from the nearest road. The son would finish the journey alone. Dad and the rest of the family would meet him at Mt. Katahdin in a few months. After a tearful embrace at the shelter, the son bravely trudged on alone.

After an hour or so at the shelter, my friend mustered up the strength to hike his final mile to the road, where he would hitchhike into town and call his wife. His eyes blurred by tears, he slowly marched down the trail, savoring each step, knowing they marked the end of his adventure.

As he rounded the final curve before he reached the road, he saw what looked to be a man in the distance, waiting. It looked an awful lot like his son. It was. He approached his son cautiously and asked him what he was still doing there. His son looked him in the eye and said, "We began this trip together and we'll finish it together. Let's go home."

Those words would haunt them for the next several years.

The following week his son went in for a routine checkup. It turned out to be anything but routine. He was immediately shuffled between doctors' offices and the hospital for further blood tests, X-rays, and a CAT scan. The battery of tests confirmed their fears. He had brain cancer of the worst kind. Because it was a very aggressive strain, the doctor said they would have to start treatments immediately to save his life.

Had the son stayed on the trail for even two more weeks, the doctor said, he would have died.

Hindsight.

The suffering of the father led to the saving of the son.

There's always more going on behind the scenes.

Like there was for Job, there's always a chapter 1 in our life that's hidden from us. Only in hindsight, after the storm has passed, can we get a glimpse of the glory of God in our suffering. But it may take years, even decades, to get that glimpse. For some of us, even a lifetime.

The truth is, none of us this side of heaven will know all that God was up to. We have to learn to wait, to be patient. This is part of the perfecting work God is determined to bring about in our lives. Spiritual hindsight does not come quickly, so don't get in a big hurry to understand everything right now.

Because it could be awhile.

Your Story

The randomness of suffering can seem meaningless. Do you see how finding meaning from God's perspective can help you find comfort?

Is it possible that in your darkest hour, God was actually hiding you with his hand, protecting you from things you couldn't see?

Can you see how your pain and suffering has benefited others?

Do you feel like there is a chapter (or chapters) of your life that is hidden from you?

23

Why God Is Never on Time

> What strength do I have, that I should still
>   hope?
> What prospects, that I should be patient?
>
> Job 6:11

I am not a patient man.

Waiting doesn't come easy to me. In fact, I hate it. I'm the guy who carefully (but in a split second) evaluates every checkout line at the grocery store to determine which one will move the fastest. Then I pounce on it, happily charging in front of the little old lady who saw it the same time I did, without even a twinge of guilt. And I'm not above jumping back and forth between lines if that's what it takes to retain my "wait less" edge.

Waiting in traffic is especially difficult for me. When I'm coming up to a red light, I find myself counting the cars in each lane to determine which one is shortest. In addition to counting the cars, as I get nearer I begin to assess the drivers in each car. Are they old? Are they young? What gender? Are they on the phone?

Are they in a Buick from Indiana? (Notoriously slow drivers by the way, if you didn't already know.)

I'm a sick man and I need help.

God knows that and stands ready to help. One of the glimpses I got during our perfect storm was this: God is never in a hurry. This is not particularly comforting when you're going through a major ordeal in life, but it's true.

God's never in a hurry and he's never on time. Because he's not *on* time or *in* time. God lives outside of time. We live in a world that is bound by time and space. We're very aware of time. And for people like me, we're aware that time's a wastin'.

But God never "wastes" time. He's always at work. Jesus affirmed that when some religious folk complained about him working on the Sabbath day. He said, "My Father is always at his work to this very day, and I, too, am working" (John 5:17).

Our heavenly Father and Jesus are always at work. They just don't seem to be in a big hurry about it.

Think about the big picture for just a minute. From Adam and Eve's first sin to the time Jesus died on the cross was somewhere around four thousand years, give or take, depending on which history scholar you talk to. (Yes I know, it could have been a lot longer, but let's use four thousand for the sake of argument.) But God promised all the way back in the Garden of Eden that he was going to provide a Redeemer who would crush the head of Satan. My guess is that Adam and Eve thought it would be sometime during their lifetime.

Nope.

Not for four thousand years. Seems like a really long time to come through on a promise. But look at what Scripture says: "You see, at just the right time, when we were still powerless, Christ died for the ungodly" (Rom. 5:6).

At just the *right* time.

Seems like a *long* time to me.

God is simply not about time like we are. He's all about the *right* time. We're all about time, but God's all about timing.

Here's the difference. Throughout the New Testament, there are two different Greek words that are translated "time." One is *chronos*, which denotes clock time such as minutes, hours, or days. The other is *kairos*, which denotes seasons or occasions. But they're both translated "time." You and I get all up in arms about *chronos*, but God is focused on *kairos*; seasons, the right time. And only he knows when that is.

But it can seem awfully slow to us.

Jesus demonstrated a serious lack of concern about *chronos* in his life on earth. You never see him running here and there, all stressed out. In fact, you never see him rushing anywhere, especially when people wanted or expected him to.

The apostle Peter says this about the pace of Jesus: "But do not forget this one thing, dear friends: With the Lord a day is like a thousand years, and a thousand years are like a day. The Lord is not slow in keeping his promise, as some understand slowness" (2 Pet. 3:8–9).

Now remember, Peter actually walked with the Lord on earth, so he's speaking from personal experience. I'm sure there were plenty of times when Peter thought Jesus was moving a little too slowly on something. In fact, I think Peter and the rest of the disciples were fairly used to Jesus being "late."

In one instance, the Feast of Tabernacles was coming up in Jerusalem. His family members were preparing to leave and, in essence, told him to hurry up and join them. A public figure like Jesus didn't need to show up late to an important function like that. But Jesus's response was, "The right time for me has not yet come; for you any time is right" (John 7:6). Jesus wasn't interested in being on time, just being there at the right time. He did finally show up at the feast, by the way.

Late.

About four days late. John records that Jesus didn't show up at the temple courts until halfway through an eight-day feast. But his timing was perfect! Had he showed up at the beginning of the feast, he'd have been arrested immediately by the authorities. They were looking for him. But by showing up several days late, he slipped in unnoticed.

Timing is everything.

But perhaps the most well-known story about Jesus being late was when he found out his buddy Lazarus was sick. Word comes to Jesus through the sisters, Mary and Martha, that Lazarus is in pretty bad shape. In other words, "We need you here. Now." Scripture records that Jesus loves Lazarus and his sisters fiercely—these were some of his very best friends in the world. But when he gets the word to come to Bethany, he stays where he is for a couple more days.

Intentionally.

There's no rush though. Certainly Jesus can heal just as well on a Friday as on a Tuesday, right? I mean, as long as Lazarus doesn't die first.

But when Jesus leaves for Bethany, Lazarus is already dead. Jesus knows it, and tells his disciples as much. By the time Jesus finally reaches Bethany, the funeral's over, the body's in the ground, and the families have gone home.

Late again.

Jesus disappointed several of his closest friends as a result. Mary and Martha are devastated. Mary is so disappointed (or more likely angry) that she doesn't even come out to greet Jesus when she hears of his arrival. When she finally does come face-to-face with Jesus, the bitterness pours out of her heart like a flood. "Lord, if you had been here, my brother would not have died" (John 11:32).

If you had been here. The implication was clear. Jesus was late. About four days too late. May as well be four thousand years. Dead is dead, after all.

But Martha's another story. You remember Martha, the workaholic sister who got a bad rap for wanting to serve Jesus, but not just hang out with him? Sadly, she's remembered most for a single, stressful moment where she lost a little perspective.

But I think Martha should be remembered for this story. In a situation where everyone around her had lost hope, she somehow found it.

Martha's disappointed, just like her sister. But she's still hopeful. Crazy hopeful. She said basically the same thing Mary did, about Jesus not being there in time to heal her brother and all. But then she demonstrates a hope that everyone else has lost. She said, "But I know that even now God will give you whatever you ask" (John 11:22). I love that! "I know that *even now* God will give you whatever you ask."

Her brother's dead, but she still has hope! Even though it's too late, she still believes "even now" that Jesus could resurrect her shattered dream, that he could restore her family, that he could raise the dead.

She's also quite practical.

After weeping profusely with the sisters, Jesus gives the command to remove the stone from the earthen tomb. Martha's first thought is, *Whoa now! His body's been in there four days. The smell might be a little overpowering.*

Always the perfect hostess.

"Then Jesus said, 'Did I not tell you that if you believed, you would see the glory of God?'" (John 11:40). Jesus said, "Stay with me. Don't give up. I know the situation stinks. But I need you to trust me on this."

"*If you will believe in me, you will see the glory of God.*"

Memorize that. Write it down and put it on your mirror. Make it a magnet and stick it on your refrigerator. Frame it in your living room.

> "*If you will believe in me, you will see the glory of God.*"

Friends, God is always up to something good because he is good. It may not come when you want it, and it may not come how you want it. But it is coming. And if we're willing to trust him, we'll see his glory! And it might be something better than a healing—it might just be a resurrection. God will reveal his glory to you in time.

And his timing is perfect. Every time.

James, another contemporary of Jesus, said this:

> Brothers, as an example of patience in the face of suffering, take the prophets who spoke in the name of the Lord. As you know, we consider blessed those who have persevered. You have heard of Job's perseverance and have seen what the Lord finally brought about. The Lord is full of compassion and mercy. (James 5:10–11)

I love the way he said that, "what the Lord *finally* brought about." In other words, it took time—a long time. But until that time comes, things can pretty much look like a disaster.

Your Story

Do you struggle with waiting? How focused do you think you are on time versus timing?

Have you ever thought God was a little late in responding to your need?

Have you been able to maintain hope even though others around you have lost hope?

Where in your life is God inviting you to believe in him so that one day you can see his glory?

24

Clever Disasters

The kingdom of God advances through a series of glorious victories cleverly disguised as disasters.

author unknown

There's a story in John 9 that's a little disconcerting to me. As Jesus travels along with his disciples, they see a man begging by the side of the road. He's blind and he's been that way all his life: blind from birth. Jesus is about twenty-five years too late on this one. This man has never seen the incredible majesty of God's creation. Never witnessed the glory of a sunrise or sunset. Never experienced the joy of seeing a rainbow after a storm. Never seen the beauty of a woman.

Never even seen himself.

Nothing.

His life is darkness, stumbling out to the road each day to beg, hoping that he can get enough spare change to feed himself that day. It's beyond sad; it's pathetic.

The guy's life is a disaster.

The prevailing theology of the day (once again) was that bad things happen to bad people, or at least people with bad parents. Based on that understanding, Jesus's disciples ask, "Rabbi, who sinned, this man or his parents, that he was born blind?" (John 9:2). In other words, "Since this guy's life is so bad, who blew it? Did he sin? What about his parents? Did they sin? I mean, for it to be this bad, somebody is to blame!"

The question lingers in the air for a moment. The stage is set. Jesus has an opportunity to set the record straight once and for all. To give us a glimpse of God's perspective when bad things happen to good people.

To tell us the reason why.

Brace yourself.

The disciples (and the blind man) lean in to hear the answer. "'Neither this man nor his parents sinned,' said Jesus, 'but this happened so that the work of God might be displayed in his life'" (John 9:3).

> *"'Neither this man nor his parents sinned,' said Jesus, 'but this happened so that the work of God might be displayed in his life'" (John 9:3).*

Come again?

This happened so the work of God could be displayed? From my perspective, I can think of a thousand better ways for God to display his work than for a man to live his entire life in darkness. I imagine the disciples were puzzled. *Hmm. No one sinned. Good guy. Born blind. Never seen the light of day. Seems a bit unfair.*

Imagine how the blind man felt!

I mean, how would you feel if you just found out you've lived your entire life in pitch-black darkness so that "God's work will somehow be displayed in your life"?

Honored? Grateful? Comforted?

Probably not.

More like confused, cheated, and perhaps a wee bit angry. Maybe a lot angry.

On top of all that, Jesus now presents the blind man with a test of faith. *Because being blind wasn't enough?* He spits on the ground, makes some mud with the dirt and saliva, and rubs it into the man's eyes. Not a pretty picture. Then he tells the man—who still can't see jack, by the way—to go across town and wash the mud off in a pool. He doesn't even offer to go with him to help him find it.

Again, I'm trying to imagine what the blind man might be thinking. *Okay, the spitting thing was pretty gross, but rubbing it into my eyes just added insult to injury. Now you want me to pick my way across town, by myself, to find a pool and wash it off? Couldn't you just say, "Be healed!" or something? It'd be a whole lot easier, not to mention faster.*

The blind man, just like you and me, is faced with a decision: to believe or not to believe. To trust God even though, thus far, nothing has gotten any better. He's still blind, for heaven's sake! He just has a dirtier face.

Talk about a journey of faith.

This story reminds me of one of my own seasons of blindness. Not physical blindness but spiritual blindness, a soul darkness when I couldn't see my way ahead anymore. It was after we had resigned the church in Huntsville and moved to Colorado, where we prayed and prayed for God to help us, but no help came. We were still depressed and without financial support, and faced the prospect of having to move back to Huntsville with our tails between our legs.

Failure.

Because of all the unanswered questions and prayers in my

life, I found myself in the dark, paralyzed, afraid to trust my-self, afraid to trust God, afraid to move forward. It was in that season that God gave me this verse: "Let him who walks in the dark, who has no light, trust in the name of the LORD and rely on his God" (Isa. 50:10).

When we can't see, that's when we learn to trust God. I thought I trusted God for everything, but when I was faced with darkness, I began to realize that my trust was based on what he did for me—or better said, what I could see that he did for me. But God doesn't want me to trust him based on what he does or doesn't do on my behalf. He wants me to simply trust him.

This is exactly the scenario the blind man is faced with. Jesus hasn't actually done anything for him yet, but he makes the decision to believe and stepping uncertainly, sets off for the pool. He's walking in complete darkness, but he's trusting Jesus.

This happened so that the work of God might be displayed in my life.

He finds the pool, washes his eyes, and comes home seeing for the very first time! He leaves in the dark, but walks home in the light.

But that's not the end of the story. His healing is only the beginning of the work that God wants to display through his life. He ends up becoming one of the first missionaries to proclaim Christ to the Jews.

Here's an interesting piece of trivia about this story you may not know. The pool where Jesus sent him was called "The Pool of Siloam." The word Siloam means "sent." So Jesus literally sent him to the pool called *sent*. He was a sent man. A missionary, by definition, is someone "who has been sent." After this man receives his sight, he becomes the first disciple of Jesus Christ to stand before the religious rulers and proclaim the glory of God.

The work of God was displayed in his life. Through his pain. Through his suffering. And through his healing. What looked like a cosmic disaster turned out to be a glorious victory for the kingdom of God.

Clever indeed.

In the same way, God will display his work and his glory in our lives through our times of trouble and loss and failure. Maybe even through our death.

There's a compelling story in the final chapter of John's Gospel when Jesus tells Peter about a storm that's coming in his future. He basically tells Peter that at the end of the day, he's going to die in a very bad way. There's a reason he is telling Peter this. "Jesus said this to indicate the kind of death by which Peter would glorify God" (John 21:19). In other words, he tells Peter that the work of God is going to be displayed in his life through his death.

Doesn't seem quite fair to Peter.

Peter's response is typical of most of us. He turns around and looks at "the disciple Jesus loved," and asks, "What about him? How's he going to die?" You know, for a point of comparison, maybe.

"Jesus answered, 'If I want him to remain alive until I return, what is that to you? You must follow me'" (John 21:22).

Jesus simply said, "What's it to you? You must follow me." In other words, Jesus tells Peter he doesn't need to compare his life, his struggles, his suffering, or even his death to anyone else. He's on a unique journey with God and his focus needs to be on following Christ—focusing on his journey, not someone else's.

In a similar way, when we're going through a major storm in life, there's a temptation to compare the intensity of our storm to someone else's storm (or lack thereof). It doesn't seem fair, so we can begin to see God as unfair or unjust "in comparison."

But Jesus says, in essence, that this is none of our concern. We're still to follow him, to focus our attention on walking with God through our storm, regardless of how unfair it seems in comparison to others. God desires for us to focus on his faithfulness, not fairness. He's promised to be with us and that's enough.

One of Job's primary complaints during his perfect storm was the unfairness of it all. He laments, "He would crush me with a storm and multiply my wounds for no reason" (Job 9:17). From Job's perspective, this all happened for no apparent reason. But the key word is *apparent*. There was no reason that he could see. He had no idea what was going on in the spiritual realm.

Job's story is a living-color example of the truth. "This happened so that the work of God might be displayed in his life," both on earth and in heaven. Here's what I mean: Remember chapter 1, the interaction between Satan and God? What was Satan's argument about why Job was doing right? Because God was taking care of him, allowing him to prosper circumstantially. In other words, "Job's only worshiping you because he's got it made. But you let Job run into a little trouble, and he'll turn on you so fast it'll make your head spin."

> *What is the greater testament to God's greatness in our lives? Worshiping God in victory, or persevering in suffering?*

Ultimately, Satan was saying he believed human beings would only love God, only trust God, and only have faith if things go well. So Satan wants to remove the material, relational, and physical prosperity, believing that Job will turn on God and lose his faith. Satan is proven wrong and God is proven right through Job's suffering. In heaven and on earth.

This poses an important question for us: What is the greater testament to God's greatness in our lives? Worshiping God in victory, or persevering in suffering? Again, it's easy to worship God when things are good. But it's a far greater testimony to the unbelieving world to trust God, to worship him, and to keep following him when things are bad. It is one of the most powerful ways God displays his work in our lives.

Speaking of Fair . . .

If you're going through an incredibly hard time right now, you've probably had at least a fleeting thought, *This is so not fair.*

And you're right. It's not.

But you may as well get used to it. As long as you and I live on planet Earth, we're not going to experience fair. However there are two sides to that: one we like, and one we don't.

One of Job's primary complaints about his life *after the storm hit* was that it was all so unfair. True.

But it makes me wonder. How much did he ponder "fair" when he was healthy, wealthy, and wise? Did he think it was fair that he had ten sons and daughters when others were childless? Was it fair that he had tremendous influence in his culture while others had no voice? Was it fair that he was one of the wealthiest men of his time while others were dirt poor?

Let's make it a little more personal. How much do you and I reflect on "fair" when things are going well? John the Baptist once said, "A man can receive only what is given him from heaven" (John 3:27). In truth, every good thing we have ever enjoyed has been given to us by God. Not because we deserved it but because of God's grace.

The whole meaning of the word *grace* is God's unmerited favor in our lives. In fact, heaven is only made possible for us through the "unfairness" of God. Scripture reminds us that

"God made him who had no sin to be sin for us, so that in him we might become the righteousness of God" (2 Cor. 5:21). Jesus was completely sinless, but he took our sin and its penalty, and exchanged it for the righteousness of God.

Now that's unfair.

The only reason we have a home in heaven is because God is unfair. That got me thinking. Because life on earth is unfair, and life in heaven is unfair, there's really only one place that a person can expect to get "fair."

It's called hell. If a person insists on fair, it seems one day they can have it.

I've decided I don't want fair. I want grace. The grace of God that allows eternal life. And the grace of God that, for now, allows suffering. I have only seen a small portion of the work of God displayed in my life so far. My story is still being written, as is yours.

But the book of Job gives us something we don't have in our lives yet: the benefit of the last chapter.

Your Story

Put yourself in the blind man's shoes. How would you feel, honestly, if you heard Jesus say your blindness existed so the work of God could be displayed in your life?

Why do you think Jesus didn't just touch the blind man's eyes and heal him instantly? What do you suppose he was teaching him? What is he teaching you?

Which do you find yourself pondering more: the fairness of God or the faithfulness of God?

Can you see how persevering in suffering is a more powerful testament to God's greatness than worshiping in victory?

25

Happily Ever After?

Though you have made me see troubles, many
and bitter,
you will restore my life again;
from the depths of the earth
you will again bring me up.
You will increase my honor
and comfort me once again.

Psalm 71:20–21

You and I have been given a great gift in the book of Job. We
have the benefit of chapter 1 and chapter 42. In chapter 1, we're
given the chance to peer behind the veil that shrouds this earth
and see what's going on in heaven. But we've also been given the
last chapter, a chance to see how it all turned out down here.
Job would be the most depressing story in Scripture if we only
had chapters 2 through 41!

But we don't. We have the rest of the story. Here's how the
storm ends.

It seems that, at the end of the day, God wasn't at all upset with Job's honest confessions about how he felt while enduring his new normal. However, Scripture records that God was a little unhappy with Job's three friends because of their insistence that a loving, just God would never let anything like this happen to a righteous man. So he tells them to offer a sacrifice to atone for their sin (which, by the way, is what they wanted Job to do all along) and then tells Job to pray for them! That's probably the best thing you can do when your friends don't get it, either. Then Scripture says this:

> After Job had prayed for his friends, the LORD made him prosperous again and gave him twice as much as he had before. All his brothers and sisters and everyone who had known him before came and ate with him in his house. They comforted and consoled him over all the trouble the LORD had brought upon him, and each one gave him a piece of silver and a gold ring.
>
> The LORD blessed the latter part of Job's life more than the first. He had fourteen thousand sheep, six thousand camels, a thousand yoke of oxen and a thousand donkeys. And he also had seven sons and three daughters. The first daughter he named Jemimah, the second Keziah and the third Keren-Happuch. Nowhere in all the land were there found women as beautiful as Job's daughters, and their father granted them an inheritance along with their brothers.
>
> After this, Job lived a hundred and forty years; he saw his children and their children to the fourth generation. And so he died, old and full of years. (Job 42:10–17)

And Job lived happily ever after. The end.

Gee, what a great finish! Everything Job lost, he got back again. His health, his wealth, his influence, his friends and family. It's almost too good to be true. I mean, this is the stuff of fairy tales.

Brace yourself.

Chances are, your storm won't end that well.

I don't mean to be discouraging, but we all must realize that the story of Job is a story of extraordinary loss and of extraordinary restoration *in this life*. I've lost children, but I've never lost ten children at the same time. I've had bad health, but I've never been disabled for any length of time. I've had my share of financial struggles, but I've never lost everything. And by the same token, I've never experienced quite the extent of restoration that Job experienced. At least not yet. Again, my story is still being told.

Bottom line: this is no time for comparison. Our story is different from Job's story. Jesus simply says to each of us, "What's that to you? You must follow me." However, there are a couple of things I need to point out in Job's story that will be true for us.

First, it *looks* like Job got everything back, but he didn't, not really. He never got his ten children back. He just got different ones. Don't you think there were days when Job mourned the loss of his previous children, wondering what they'd be like now and longing to go back? I believe he shed tears for years to come, just like you and me.

Second, take a closer look at the phrase that starts this passage: "after he prayed." There's a temptation to think this all happened very quickly, but in reality it was over a long, long period of time. I mean, it's going to take at least ten years to have ten more children. I think Job's health gradually got better, his friends and family slowly started showing up again, and he rebuilt his family business one transaction at a time. My point is this: it takes a long, long time to rebuild your life after a major tragedy. It's never quick and it's never easy. God wants us to learn perseverance in the process.

The Rest of the Story

Years ago there was a popular radio show hosted by Paul Harvey called *The Rest of the Story*. Every week, Paul would give his listeners the benefit of knowing the story behind the story. He'd tell a little of a famous story, the part everyone already knew, but then he'd take the time to tell the back story, the part of the story almost no one knew. And it was often about how something incredibly good came out of something incredibly bad.

I loved that show. I always want to know how things turn out. You probably do too. In addition to my own story, I've shared the stories of several other people throughout this book. Now let me tell you "the rest of their stories."

I spoke of a family whose daughter was raped in her first year at college. Through the love and support of her family and friends, that daughter has experienced incredible healing and forgiveness. She's now married to a wonderful Christian man and they just gave birth to a beautiful baby girl. She loves the Lord, and she and her husband share the dream of doing ministry together.

I told you the story of a young couple who held on to God and each other and survived the husband's major bout with cancer only to see their new dreams disintegrate when their house burned to the ground. They have since rebuilt a brand-new house, and now the young man is studying to be a nurse so he can provide the same kind of care and healing for others he received during his cancer ordeal. (You thought he was going to be a firefighter, didn't you?)

Knowing that the brutal cancer treatments would render him sterile, the young man and his then-fiancée exercised a little foresight and cryogenically preserved a sperm sample. By the grace of God, and a little technological help, he and his wife recently presented their grateful parents with twin grandchildren, a boy and a girl.

And I told you about my good friend who introduced me to the whole concept of the new normal, the father whose son had inoperable brain cancer. They found out about the cancer only after giving up their dream of finishing the Appalachian Trail together. You might recall what the son said that day: "We started this together, and we'll finish it together."

To God's glory, after several years of treatment and rehabilitation, father and son went back out on the trail together, picked up where they left off, and finished their thru hike of the AT. Atop Mount Katahdin that final day, they enjoyed a tearful reunion with the entire family.

My friend and his wife have since started a ministry for other AT thru hikers, providing fresh-cooked food and beverages for weary hikers at strategic points along the trail. They listen to their stories, knowing from experience that every person has a story to tell. And when God gives them the opportunity, they tell their story of walking the trail of life alongside the God who allows suffering.

By the way, there's common denominator in all three of those stories.

It's the same family.

Seriously. My good friend is a modern-day Job. My wife and I have been privileged to walk with them from the day they received each dreadful phone call of fire and cancer and rape, all the way to sharing a vacation with them this past summer, enjoying their children and three beautiful grandchildren.

I hope I've been a better friend than Job's were.

Are my friends living happily ever after? Well, yes and no. They have much to be thankful for, to be sure. They enjoy seasons with their family and friends, hiking, fishing, and spending the holidays together. But they also go through long periods of depression, trying to grasp what happened to the life they once knew, longing for the innocence they lost to a series of storms. But their story isn't finished. God continues to write new chapters in their life; some they'll like, and others not so much. But in the end, they'll all be good chapters.

Where Dreams Are Born

Several years ago, at a Catalyst conference in Atlanta, I heard a guy named Wintley Phipps sing. I'd never heard of him before the conference, but he shared something that day I will never forget:

> It is in the quiet crucible of your personal private sufferings that your noblest dreams are born and God's greatest gifts are given, in compensation for [what] you've been through.

I wrote that one down! I took a lot of notes that week, but this one I circled and highlighted. *God's noblest dreams and greatest gifts come through suffering.* Mr. Phipps sang the song "Amazing Grace" that day, but I have since found out that he often sings another song in conjunction with that quote: "It Is Well with My Soul."

Which brings us to the rest of another story, that of Horatio and Anna Spafford. You know, the couple who saw much of their wealth go up in smoke in the Great Chicago Fire, lost all four daughters in a shipwreck, and then lost their only son to scarlet fever. Most people know that Horatio went on to write the beloved hymn "It Is Well with My Soul." But what most people don't know is how God worked through this couple *after* their season of loss.

They had two more daughters born to them after their tragedies. You'll love the name of their youngest.

Grace.

Almost unbelievably, after all of their trials, the name they chose for their final child reflected their steadfast trust in the grace of God. In 1881, they left the relative comfort of Chicago and moved their small family to Jerusalem to do philanthropic work among the poor in the holy city. Is it any surprise their focus was on the children? The Spaffords started an orphanage that has served more than thirty thousand children since its inception. The Spafford Children's Center continues to provide medical care and other programs for children and their families in Jerusalem to this day.

God's noblest dreams are born through suffering.

Your story isn't finished yet either. God will continue to write new chapters in your life, in his time and according to his purposes. And don't be surprised if God uses your worst suffering to birth a vision in you that will be of great benefit to others. That's often what it takes to see beyond ourselves.

Your Story

Do you find comfort in how Job's story resolves, or does it frustrate you a little bit?

Do you think there could be a correlation between the extraordinary losses the Spaffords experienced and their extraordinary sacrifices later in life?

How has your perspective on life changed as a result of your suffering?

What dreams might God be birthing in your own heart that will allow your pain to benefit others?

26

God Has Remembered Us

I know that you can do all things;
no plan of yours can be thwarted.

Job 42:2

At the end of the day, Job acknowledges that God has a cosmic plan going on, a plan that will work itself out in time. Job couldn't see what it was at the time any more than we can, but he learned to trust God's ability as an architect, knowing from experience that God always writes the last chapter. This thread of providential grace through suffering is woven throughout Scripture and most of us can find our own story hidden in those pages too.

There are two stories told in the Old Testament about women who couldn't have children. Rachel's story is told in Genesis 30 and Hannah's story in 1 Samuel 1. While their stories are different, they share several similarities. Both women suffered disgrace for a long period of time as a result of not being able to have children. And in both stories, when God miraculously provided each woman a son, Scripture records that God "remembered" them. It's not that God ever actually "forgot" them, but because it took so long, from a human perspective, it sure felt that way.

What I love about Wintley Phipps's quote is that not only are God's noblest dreams born but also *his greatest gifts* given through suffering. My wife and I came to know this from personal experience.

I have one final story to tell you—ours. I told you the story of how we lost the twins, but what I didn't tell you is what happened two weeks later.

Here's the rest of our story.

After we put Dawn on a plane back to her previous home with twin sons we had hoped would be ours, we tried to settle into our new normal. I was emotionally exhausted and cynical, but trying to be supportive as my wife began the task of "undoing" a nursery designed for two. It was a Saturday morning and I was lounging on the couch, reflecting on the last nine months or so of our life. I had no answers for any of it.

The phone rang.

I'd reached the point where I really didn't care for the phone, and I sure didn't feel like answering it that day. But I did, just in case it was a member of our congregation who might be in some kind of crisis that demanded pastoral support.

Not that I had much to give.

It was a female voice I recognized as my sister's friend. She told me that she knew a twenty-one-year-old single mom with three kids who was pregnant with her fourth. She knew she couldn't care for another child and had asked this friend to contact us.

She wanted to give us her baby.

Yeah, right. Been there, done that, currently wearing the T-shirt.

She gave us a number to call. *Great, another phone call.* Everything in me didn't want to tell my wife, but since she was in the room, there was no way to avoid it. Marlina was cautiously excited, but I was just tired of the whole thing. I reluctantly dialed the number, hoping to sound enthusiastic as I interacted with yet another birthmother, whom we'll call Kim. A male voice answered. I explained that I wanted to talk to Kim about her baby. The male voice on the other end of the line said defensively, "If you want to talk to Kim about her baby, you can just talk to me!"

Oh, great. I've got the birthfather on the line and they haven't been talking.

I hung up the phone.

I was done. There was no way I was going down this dead-end road again.

Marlina was appalled. She couldn't believe what I'd just done. More than appalled, she was angry. At me. How could I even think of jeopardizing this God-given opportunity to have a child?

The phone rang again.

This time, I took the initiative. I was going to lead my wife and protect her from additional hurt. This guy had dialed *69 and apparently wanted to finish the conversation I had abruptly ended. "Don't you dare answer that phone!" I said, bristling. At which point, my dear, sweet, submissive wife did what any woman would do in the same situation.

She answered the phone.

That male voice wasn't the birthfather—it was the grand-father. Not surprisingly, he liked talking to Marlina a whole lot better. She didn't hang up the phone or anything rash like that. God gave her tremendous favor in their conversation, and the grandfather gave her Kim's number. Another phone call.

Here we go again.

Later, Marlina talked to Kim and found out she was due to have the baby in just a few weeks. She hadn't been to a doctor, but she was confident of her due date. Realizing that time was of the essence, I got on the phone with our lawyer.

We got Kim set up for a doctor's appointment and found out that she and the baby were healthy. However, the doctor assured us she was still two months away from delivery. We'd been planning a much-needed vacation, so we went ahead with our plans, knowing we had plenty of time before the baby arrived.

On Saturday night, we finished packing the car for a trip to Florida. I was more than ready to get out of town, away from all this madness. I would preach in the morning and then we'd head for the beach.

God had a different plan. Turns out, a better one.

About three in the morning, our phone rang. Kim was at the hospital and she was having the baby.

We threw on some clothes, and I put in a call to our co-pastor to ask if he could be ready to preach in about six hours! (I think I said something about being ready in season and out of season. . . .) It was still pitch-dark as we jumped in the car, a mixture of excitement and uncertainty in our hearts. Would Kim really be able to go through with it? Could any mother give up her child to near-total strangers?

Dawn was breaking as we walked into the hospital and were directed to the labor and delivery waiting room. There was only one baby in the newborn area, a boy, and we peered through the glass, wondering if this could be a new addition to our family. We took out our camera and began to take a few pictures of this child just in case.

Suddenly a very stern-faced nurse came out the door and told us to stop. She informed us this was a "Baby Doe," and no pictures could be taken without parental permission. At that point we were pretty sure this was Kim's baby, but we didn't know what to make of the "Baby Doe" status. Had Kim changed her mind?

We obediently sat back down, not wanting to mess anything up. I remember feeling a mixture of irritation and fear. *Why does this have to be so hard? We've come this far and now we're forbidden to take pictures . . . of our own son.*

As I was a recovering control freak, this was pushing every one of my buttons. *Hold it together, Bruce. Don't blow it. Smile and say the right things.*

About an hour later another nurse rounded the corner, and with a reassuring smile asked us, "Would you like to see your baby?" Marlina practically exploded out of her seat. We followed the nurse back to the newborn baby area where she confided to us that Kim had already signed over parental rights and wanted to transfer the "mother's wristband" to Marlina, giving us complete access to our new son. The nurse wrapped the wristband around Marlina's wrist, then handed her a beautiful baby boy, the same one we had taken pictures of just an hour earlier. It was surreal, watching Marlina look down into that child's face as only a mother can. Her dream of being a mom was finally realized.

God had remembered her.

The next week was full of both joy and sorrow. Much to our surprise, Kim was ready to go home within hours of delivery. She asked for one more chance for her and her dad, the baby's grandfather, to see the child. It was a bittersweet moment as I watched this young mother kiss her child for the final time. But that wasn't the hardest thing to watch. After the grandfather said his good-byes, he began sobbing. Not just crying, but sobbing, his lungs taking in great gulps of air then expelling it in staccato heaves. He motioned for my wife to come near and tried to speak between sobs. Over and over again, he said, "Please tell me you'll take good care of him. Please!" The desperation in his voice was more than I could take.

It was truly the saddest thing I had ever seen.

I remember thinking how wrong this whole picture was. What should have been one of the happiest days of my life was filled with so much sorrow that the emotional juxtaposition was almost too much to bear. I left the room as quickly as I could and went back to the waiting room. It had several people in it now, so I snuck into the children's area, which was vacant and dark, and curled up on the floor underneath a play table. I wanted to cry, but I couldn't. The tears just wouldn't come. I shut my eyes and finally drifted off to sleep, not caring if anyone knew where I was or not. I didn't really want to be found.

I didn't get to sleep long. Within hours of our holding him for the first time, our son was whisked away again. There were problems. He had fluid built up in his lungs and the doctor was concerned about poor lung formation. For the next five days he was in intensive care and we could only see him twice a day. It was painfully hard to see him all alone in a clear chamber with hoses and tubes going everywhere. He needed to be held, to be touched. To bond with his new parents. Thankfully, we had some wonderful nurses who let us hold him twice a day and feed him.

Our stress level was off the charts all week. We couldn't go home, so we stayed with my parents, who happened to live in that city, so we could make daily trips to the ICU. Good thing we already had the car packed for a weeklong trip!

On our son's last night in the hospital, the doctors wanted us to stay with him in a private room. If everything went well, we could take him home the following day. He was still hooked up to all kinds of monitors, which went off at all hours of the night, kind of like fire alarms. We kept expecting a nurse to rush in and take him away again, but no one came. As new parents, we didn't sleep a wink, but kept our eyes on him and the computer screens all night. It was wonderful and awful at the same time.

After leaving the hospital with our son, we stayed with my parents one more day, just in case. The following day we made the trip home to Alabama to share our gift with friends and family there.

We decided to name our new son Zachary. It comes from the Hebrew name *Zechariah*, and means "God has remembered us." After years of fertility nightmares, frustrating home studies, legal fees out the wazoo, and a failed adoption, we finally had a child.

God remembered our suffering and gave us our greatest earthly gift.

Now, let me tell you why the birthmother, Kim, decided to contact us in the first place. She had heard the story from her friend about how we had lost the twins and made the decision *that day* to give us her child. She never wavered. She felt like God wanted her to give us this child.

Had we never experienced the painful loss of the twins, we'd never have known the joy of Zachary.

Hindsight.

I've come to understand that this mixture of joy and sorrow, sometimes felt simultaneously, is normal in this life. God calls us to drink deeply from the cup of rejoicing and the cup of suffering. In fact, they're the same cup.

It's called hope.

And we rejoice in the hope of the glory of God. Not only so, but we also rejoice in our sufferings, because we know that suffering produces perseverance; perseverance, character; and character, hope. And hope does not disappoint us, because God has poured out his love into our hearts by the Holy Spirit, whom he has given us. (Rom. 5:2–5)

Hope does not disappoint us, because God has poured out his love.

I smile as I write this. My son Zach is a fearless and energetic teenager now. He loves hiking, golf, football, skateboards, motorcycles, and anything extreme. Just like his dad. When people see him with me for the first time, they always say the same thing: "I can tell he's your son. He looks just like you!" I don't even try to explain that he's adopted. No one believes me.

By the grace of God, I fathered a son with my DNA after all. And he's more than I hoped for.

Your Story

Have you been in pain for so long that it feels like God has forgotten you? Have you given up hope?

The birth of my son was one of the happiest and saddest days of my life. Are you coming to understand that both joy and sorrow are part of God's plan for your life?

Scripture teaches that hoping is not having. How do you feel about hoping for something that you may never experience in this life?

Hope does not disappoint because God has poured out his love in our hearts. Is God's love enough?

27

God's Will and Suffering

They comforted and consoled him over all the
trouble the LORD had brought upon him.

Job 42:11

There's a statement in the passage about Job's restoration, almost hidden in the narrative, that creates more questions than answers. It's the phrase "all the trouble the Lord had brought upon him." It begs the question that inevitably comes up in the conversation about bad things happening to good people: "Was this God's will?" The writer of Job doesn't try to gloss over it or explain it away. He just accepts, as Job did, that both good and bad come from the hand of the Lord.

You and I could argue, because of what we are privy to in chapter 1, that Satan was the one who brought all the trouble on Job. But then again, God could've stopped him. So God, at the very least, *allowed* Job to suffer. Which brings us back to the question: Was this God's will?

Let's personalize it a little bit. How about your storm—your loss, your pain, your suffering, your betrayal? Was it God's will? I have the definitive answer for you.

I don't know.

Frankly, it's way above my pay grade. Some very good Christians, who are a lot smarter than I am, argue that because God is sovereign his will is always being done. Period. End of discussion. Everything that happens is God's will. So if someone is sinned against—raped, murdered, oppressed—it's God's will. Perhaps they're right.

But I'm not so sure, partly because of Jesus's teaching on prayer. In probably the most famous discussion of prayer, what we typically call "The Lord's Prayer," Jesus instructs us to pray for God's will to "be done on earth just as it is in heaven." To me that at least engages the possibility, if not outright assumes, that God's will is not always being done on earth. In heaven, God's will is being effected perfectly. But the very fact that Jesus told us to pray for God's will to be done "on earth" seems to indicate that a person can make choices that are not God's will.

At the same time, there's a bunch of Scriptures that indicate it is the will of God that we experience suffering. So how do we deal with the tension? Well, Peter simply says it this way: "It is better, if it is God's will, to suffer for doing good than for doing evil" (1 Pet. 3:17). In other words, the will of God includes suffering for doing wrong and for doing right. But if you are going to suffer, it's better to suffer for doing what's right.

Peter also said, "But if you suffer for doing good and you endure it, this is commendable before God. To this you were called, because Christ suffered for you, leaving you an example, that you should follow in his steps" (1 Pet. 2:20–21). Suffering is simply part of our calling; it's part of following Christ.

I don't really like that.

But this is why I say that God is more intent on perfecting us through suffering than he is on protecting us from suffering. I know from experience that suffering brings a certain kind of spiritual fruit that nothing else can. One of these fruits is humility. One of the things God showed me during one of my seasons of suffering is how much pride was in my heart. I remember reading the story of King Hezekiah, told in Isaiah 36–38, and realizing his story was my story in many ways. King Hezekiah was a very successful king, but Scripture records that he became proud in the process. So God brought a perfect storm into his life that included being vastly outnumbered in a war with the Assyrian army and contracting a terminal illness at the same time.

A humbling position to be in—out of control, about to lose everything. But God delivers him, eventually, and on the other side of his storm, he pens these words:

> But what can I say?
>   He has spoken to me, and he himself has done this.
> I will walk humbly all my years
>   because of this anguish of my soul.
> Lord, by such things men live;
>   and my spirit finds life in them too.
> You restored me to health
>   and let me live.
> Surely it was for my benefit
>   that I suffered such anguish.
> In your love you kept me
>   from the pit of destruction;
> you have put all my sins
>   behind your back. (Isa. 38:15–17)

Did you catch his take on his suffering?

"He himself has done this."

"I will walk humbly all my years."

"By such things men live."

"Surely it was for my benefit."

Hezekiah acknowledged that his suffering was for his benefit. He learned humility, the humility of trusting God instead of trusting himself. It's what life is really about: trusting God. As I read Hezekiah's story, I had to acknowledge the same. By such things men live, and my spirit finds life in them too. I pray that I will walk humbly for the rest of my life because of the anguish of my soul.

I don't believe there are any easy answers to the question, "Was this God's will?" But one thing that has helped me navigate my own suffering is to make a distinction between the will of God and the work of God. I can trust the work of God even when I don't understand the will of God.

Again, Jesus pointed out, "My Father is always at his work to this very day" (John 5:17). I can trust that God is always up to something good, behind the scenes, working, never resting. He's doing things I can't see, at least not yet.

> *I can trust the work of God even when I don't understand the will of God.*

To that degree I've stopped trying to figure out whether something bad that happened was God's will. I don't even ask the question anymore. I simply look for the work of God in every situation. I know that God is at work, achieving through my light and momentary troubles an eternal glory that far outweighs them all (see 2 Cor. 4:17).

And I know that one day, whether in this life or the next, all things will work together for my good, because I'm loved by God and I'm designed for his purposes (see Rom. 8:28).

The Extended Forecast

If I was to sum up the "weather forecast" for the rest of our lives here on earth, I would say something like, "Sunny with severe storms likely."

The rest of your life will be a mixture of sunny days and severe storms. I'd love to tell you that you won't have to experience more storms, but there's no getting around it. It's a promise from God. Jesus said, "In this world you will have trouble." That's a promise. But he also said things like, "But don't be discouraged. I have overcome the world."

And so will we.

I've heard people who have gone through intense storms say, "I never thought I could survive something like this." But they did. God gave them exactly what they needed when the time came. That's why Jesus said, "Don't worry about tomorrow. Each day has enough trouble." Take each day as it comes, with its mixture of joy and sorrow, sunny days and storms. It's the way God chooses to perfect us.

Not only do we have the benefit of the last chapters in Job, we also have the last chapters in Hebrews. While Job finishes with an almost fairy-tale ending, Hebrews finishes with a mix of glorious victories and resounding defeats. It's a book that not only shatters the myth of a life without suffering but also the myth of everyone living "happily ever after," at least in this life. Hebrews 11 explodes once and for all the prosperity gospel notion that if we have enough faith, things will all turn out hunky-dory here and now.

Hebrews 11 is often referred to as "God's Hall of Faith." It describes some people of great faith who experience victory in battle, deliverance from trouble, healing from disease, and miraculous resurrection from the dead.

It also describes people of equally great faith who experienced defeat, insult, flogging, torture, and imprisonment. They lived as fugitives in this life and many of them died . . . badly. Stoned, sawn in two, impaled by the sword.

But all of them were commended for their faith.

The brutal reality is God doesn't promise a happy ending to all of our trials here on earth. Some people see their child healed from cancer, others watch as their child dies a slow and painful death. Some people will get their job back, others will endure a lifetime of being overqualified and underpaid.

Joy and sorrow. Victory and defeat. It's all in the life of faith.

There's a day coming when all of us will truly live "happily ever after." A day when everything and everyone will be perfect. There will be a restoration of all things. The writer of Hebrews sums up the entire chapter with this: "God had planned something better for us so that only together with us would they be made perfect" (v. 40). That day is coming, but it's not here yet. So we wait. And trust. And hope, "longing for a better country—a heavenly one" (v. 16).

The Perfect Life

By now you hopefully realize that "the perfect life" isn't exactly what you thought it was. It's not about material or physical prosperity. It's about soul prosperity. The perfect life is not some kind of legalistic, sinless perfection. I depend on the grace of God to forgive my sin struggles every day. Nor is it a life without significant trouble or disasters. The older I get, the more I realize that the perfect life is simply being loved by God every single day.

God is deeply in love with me, and no matter what I go through, good or bad, nothing will change that love.

Who shall separate us from the love of Christ? Shall trouble or hardship or persecution or famine or nakedness or danger or sword? . . . No, in all these things we are more than conquerors through him who loved us. (Rom. 8:35–37).

Turns out we can have the perfect life after all. It's also called eternal life.

In John 17, Jesus describes what eternal life is. In fact, it's the whole point of this life and the next. But it's probably not what you think. When we think of "eternal life," we think in terms of a never-ending quantity of time. But that's not how Jesus describes it at all. "Now this is eternal life: that they may know you, the only true God, and Jesus Christ, whom you have sent" (John 17:3). Did you get that? *This is eternal life—knowing you!*

It's not a quantity of life—it's a quality of life. A life of knowing God. And that's the whole point of suffering: to know God. To know Jesus. God wants us to know him! And there's nothing like suffering to move us from the point of knowing about God (information) to actually knowing God (life).

One of the greatest gifts I have been given by God through suffering is understanding the value of his presence in my life. When I am alone, I am never really alone at all. He is right there with me. I am aware of The Presence. And that brings incredible peace no matter what the circumstances. And it gives me courage. It's very different than believing nothing bad will happen to me. In fact, it embraces that reality. But I'm not alone. I will never be alone.

We make a big deal about "famous last words" in our culture. There's an understanding that at the end of everyone's life, they probably have something important to say. There's a certain kind of wisdom that can only be gleaned from a lifetime of experiences.

So what were Jesus's last words? What was the wisdom he gleaned from a lifetime of walking with his Father? What words had God used to sustain him during his years on earth? What words did he know we would desperately need to hear as we seek to carry on his mission on earth?

Your Story

Have you lost a certain amount of sleep trying to figure out if your suffering was God's will?

What are some of the character traits God is birthing (or has birthed) in your life as a result of your suffering?

Even if you can't discern his will, does it comfort you to know that God is at work "behind the scenes" for good?

What are the words you most need to hear from God right now?

Epilogue

Famous Last Words

And surely I am with you always, to the very end of the age.

Matthew 28:20

Always.
No matter what happens.
Even at the end of your world.
Jesus is with you.

Bruce W. Martin serves as Lead Follower of a new mission-driven church in Huntsville, Alabama called 100X Church (www.100xchurch.com) and also serves as president of The Cornerstone Initiative, a collaborative effort to provide a solution to generational poverty in Alabama (www.cornerstone-al.com). He is also an inspirational speaker for churches, conferences, marriage retreats, men's outings, young adult venues, and outreach events. He is uniquely gifted in connecting with churched and unchurched people alike, and is especially passionate about sharing the gospel in a variety of settings (www.brucewmartin.com).

An avid outdoorsman, Bruce has logged hundreds of back-packing miles on the Appalachian Trail and the Sierra Nevada mountain range of California. He loves to get away from the speed and noise of suburban life and get back to the basics of walking with God, hearing his voice, and enjoying him in his creation. Bruce, his wife Marlina, and their son Zachary reside in Huntsville, Alabama.